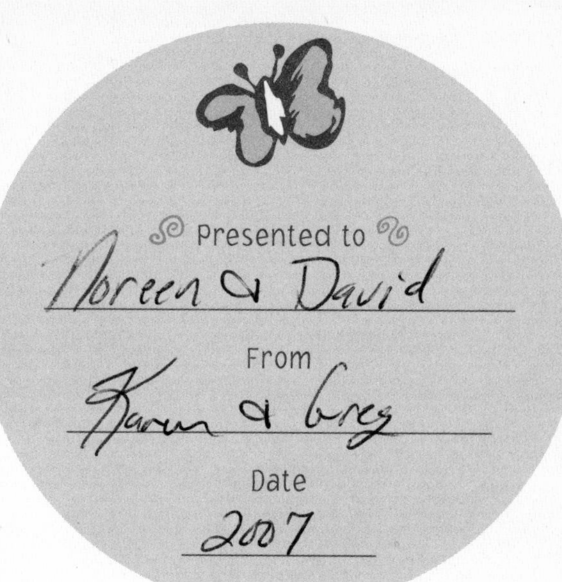
Presented to
Noreen & David
From
Karen & Greg
Date
2007

To my on-the-go family:
my husband, Joe,
and my children, Jen, Katy, and Dan

Kids Say the Best Things About God

Devotions and Conversations for Families On the Go

Dandi Daley Mackall

Published by Jossey-Bass
A Wiley Imprint
989 Market Street, San Francisco, CA 94103-1741
www.josseybass.com

Jossey-Bass books and products are available through most bookstores. To contact Jossey-Bass directly call our Customer Care Department within the U.S. at 800-956-7739, outside the U.S. at 317-572-3986, or fax 317-572-4002.

Jossey-Bass also publishes its books in a variety of electronic formats. Some content that appears in print may not be available in electronic books.

Library of Congress Cataloging-in-Publication Data

MacKall, Dandi Daley.
Kids say the best things about God: devotions and conversations for families on the go/Dandi Daley MacKall.—1st ed.
p. cm.
ISBN 0-7879-6967-2 (alk. paper)
1. Family—Prayer-books and devotions—English. I. Title.
BV255.M32 2003
249—dc22 2003016731

Printed in the United States of America

FIRST EDITION

HB Printing 10 9 8 7 6 5 4 3 2 1

Contents

✳ Introduction ✳

If your family is at all like mine, most mornings are mayhem—parents rushing to work, kids hurrying to make the bus or catch a ride to school. Evenings aren't that much calmer, with homework, ball games, piano lessons, errands, friends, favorite TV shows. Yet many families yearn for a stronger spiritual life, a closer family.

This book offers an opportunity for your family to grow spiritually, even in the midst of your crazy lives. The plan is realistic: two to five minutes together in the morning (and even those few minutes can take place over breakfast), then an on-the-go conversation at the end of the day. No preparation required. The lessons are for *all* of you. For thirty days, your family can send each other off on your separate ways with a laugh and a practical thought that will increase your awareness of Christ's presence throughout the day. Then you can share discoveries when your paths cross at the end of the day.

Each section of the book contains these features:

- *An opening quote or two from children* I gathered the quotes from children in elementary schools all across the United States. As I visited classrooms and talked about writing and life, I asked kids questions. Then I listened and wrote as fast as I could. The quotes are amusing and are followed by a related odd fact or bit of fun trivia. If you do nothing more than laugh together first thing in the morning for thirty days, your family will have taken a big step.
- *A scripture passage* This represents "What God Says" about the topic at hand, as he speaks to us through the Bible.
- *The basic thought in the lesson* "The Big Idea" builds on the day's scripture pas-

sages, expanding one main thought or lesson. One family member could read this section while the others eat breakfast.

- *Instructive questions* "Taking God with Us" includes four questions that are designed to get all of you to observe God's world in a specific way that applies to the lesson for that day.
- *Parting prayer* With a short family prayer, you're on your way!
- *End-of-the-day report* The last section asks questions to get your family talking and sharing events and discoveries of the day. You could have the discussion on the way to a ball game, over a hamburger at a fast-food place, or during a TV commercial. You could record the answers and create your own family journal.
- *A final scripture passage* A final look at God's Word should sum up, or add new light to, your family's spiritual discoveries for each day.

If you're a family on the go, frustrated because you can't gather everyone by the fireside for long devotionals each night, you can still grow spiritually as a family. You can grab the opportunities you do have and bring lasting changes as you discover more about God and more about each other.

✳ Day 1 ✳

How does God get those leaves to grow back onto the trees? And how does God keep grass growing back, no matter how many times you cut it off? Now that's something!

David, 8

SURPRISE!

Surprise! Did you know that you may have eaten grass today? Most breakfast cereals are made of some kind of grass—corn, oats, wheat, barley. Even sugar comes from sugarcane—a type of grass. Grass is just one of the daily miracles surrounding us.

Have you ever noticed the way all the leaves on a single tree open the same day, even though some leaves are in shade and others are in the sun? Or the way cows lie down before a rain, but frogs just croak louder? Listen to crickets chirp; then count the number of chirps you hear in fifteen seconds, add 37, and you've got the current temperature. Did you know that houseflies hum (rapid wing movement) in the key of F major and that a single dandelion is really a cluster of about two hundred tiny flowers?

Check it out. Pay attention. Surprises are everywhere.

What God Says

You have seen many things, but have paid no attention; your ears are open, but you hear nothing.

—Isaiah 42:20

The Big Idea

God wants our attention. We have been given a world filled with amazement and wonder at every turn. A flock of birds takes off in a flutter of wings, filling the sky with the marvel of flight. A shadow falls between trees splashed in sunlight. Moonlight hits a pile of broken glass, transforming ugly shards into sparkling diamonds.

Yet most of us go through the day without paying attention to our world, created by hand, made by God just for us. In Isaiah, the Lord shouts at people to wake up. Hear! See! Sing a new song—from the sea, to the islands, from the desert, to the mountaintops. Heads up!

Why did God bother to create colors? He could have easily created a world that could stumble along OK in black and white. But from nearly anywhere you stand today, you'll see dozens of colors. One researcher named 125 shades of blue alone!

You may be so used to your daily routine that you could get to school or to work with your eyes closed. But no trip, no day, will ever be the same. Don't miss the surprises of today. You won't get them again.

Taking God with Us

Today, on your journeys to and from school or work and during the normal routines of the day, pay attention. Expect to be surprised by God's world.

1. Look for two surprises on the way to your routine (school, work) this morning—two wonders of creation you haven't noticed or perhaps have never seen before in just this way.
2. Listen for two surprising sounds on your way to school or work—a bird, the wind, a voice.
3. During the day, notice as many surprises as you can.
4. Share at least one surprise with one other person today.

Parting Prayer

God, thank you so much for loving us enough to create a world full of beauty and enchantment, new every morning. Forgive us for taking your blessings, little and big, for granted. Help us be childlike today, filled with excitement at what you have in store. Surprise us!

Reporting on God's Surprises

Give each family member an opportunity to report on today's discoveries. One person might record all the responses. Or anyone who wishes could make a note or draw a picture of God's surprising gifts to your family today.

1. What was the best surprise you saw today on your way to work or school,

or wherever you went? Why did this sight capture your attention?

2. What was the best, most surprising sound you heard today? Do you think you've heard it before but didn't pay attention?
3. Did you share a surprise? With whom?
4. Take a look (and a listen) around you right this minute. Any surprises?

Command those who are rich in this present world . . . to put their hope in God, who richly provides us with everything for our enjoyment.

—I Timothy 6:17

Day 2

I know what makes God angry. It's when God's creations don't turn out so good, like cockroaches and my brother.

Alex, 7

OH BROTHER!

Cockroaches and brothers. And sisters. Maybe they do have things in common. Cockroaches are everywhere you don't want them to be. They've even shown up on spacecrafts! They eat everything (leather, soap, paint, glue, toothpaste, spinach, and worse). In a pinch, they'll even turn on each other and chow down. They're noisemakers. The Madagascar hissing cockroach forces air out of its breathing holes and makes a hissing squeak that drives its enemies crazy.

And you can't get rid of cockroaches. They can survive in outer space. They live in rain forests and in deserts where they never see a drop of rain. Freeze them, and they'll be fine when they thaw.

Since cockroaches (and siblings) aren't going away, guess we'll have to learn to live with them.

What God Says

Anyone who claims to be in the light but hates his brother is still in the darkness.

—I John 2:9

The Big Idea

Family is for life. As close as you are to your friends (who may be easier to get along with than family), friends may change, move away, stop being friends. Your family will always be your family.

God could have given you any brother or sister in the world. Instead, you got this exact family. For whatever reasons—and most of them we'll never know or understand—these are the people God chose for you to learn from. The problems and friction in your family help mold you and grow you into the person God wants you to become.

Sibling strife is part of the package deal we're given when we're born into a family. As Chelsea, age nine, said, "I used to wonder why we got brothers and sisters. But now I know it's so your parents don't have to spend all their time just yelling at you. And if we didn't have brothers and sisters, we'd have to fight with strangers."

Learn from each other. Pray for one another. Treat family members with at least as much respect and kindness as you treat your friends. Work at your relationship with each individual member of your family. Family is for life!

Taking God with Us

Today, when you're with your family and when you're apart, think about these people God has given you for life.

1. Why do you think God gave you your family? Take each person individually and try to understand how God is using your brother or sister or parents to mold you.
2. During the day, picture each person in your family. Try to understand how God is using you to help them grow.
3. Thank God for one specific quality or character trait in each member of your family.
4. Be prepared to tell what you like best about each person in your family, including yourself.

Parting Prayer

Father, thank you for our family. Thanks for hand-creating each of us and for moving heaven and earth to bring us together into one family. Help us to appreciate each other today. Make us aware of the way you're using us in each other's lives.

Reporting on God's Hand-Picked Family

One family member may want to start "thankful biographies" that can be added to as time goes on, listing reasons you're grateful for each other. Younger siblings could draw pictures of the family.

1. Parents, name three ways you can see how your own siblings—the family you grew up in—molded you into the person you are today.

2. Starting with the oldest sibling, family members can all share at least one reason why they think God gave them that person. Continue until everyone has been discussed.
3. How do you see yourself as essential to your family? How do you think God is using you as part of this family?
4. Have everyone complete this statement: "The best thing about being part of this family is ______________________________
______________________________."

But as for me and my household, we will serve the Lord.

—Joshua 24:15

Day 3

I can't wait to get to heaven! There are streets of gold, and you can play right out in the middle of them without getting yourself runned over! Plus, you can play on a baseball team and not be the last one picked!

Jack, 6

What do you mean Jesus is coming back? Nobody ever tells me anything!

Rudy, 7

IT'S HOW YOU LOOK AT IT

There are two ways to look at nearly everything that happens. One way leads to frustration; the other, eventually, to contentment. John Quincy Adams, second president of the

United States, suffered for two years following a stroke. When a friend asked about his health, Adams calmly reported that his body was a decayed tenement, battered by winds and broken by storms, and the Landlord didn't seem likely to do repairs. But when Adams collapsed in Congress in the winter of 1848, his final words were, "This is the last of Earth. I am content."

It's all how you look at it. Take the gross flower called stapelia. The bloom looks like dead animal skin and smells like rotting meat. Yet without that bad smell, there would be no stapelia. The particular stench attracts flies that pollinate and increase the number of flowers. Even stinking can be a good thing.

What God Says

For I have learned to be content whatever the circumstances. I have learned the secret of being content in any and every situation, whether well fed or hungry, whether living in plenty or in want.

—Philippians 4:11–12

The Big Idea

Some of the biggest complaints come from people with the least to complain about. And some of the happiest, most contented people should logically be weighed down with the load they're carrying. Contentment has more to do with attitude than with actual circumstances.

Take Paul, for example. He was an apostle. Easy for him to say he was content in all circumstances, right? But in II Corinthians 11, he lists a few of those circumstances: five times whipped thirty-nine lashes; three times beaten with rods; stoned and left for dead; shipwrecked three times; suffered dangers from rivers, from cold, from starvation and thirst, dangers from robbers, dangers from betrayal, from his own countrymen trying to kill him. If Paul had depended on circumstances to feel content, he never would have experienced contentment. His contentment grew from his friendship with God.

Our contentment comes from knowing and trusting God and being grateful for God's friendship. No matter how bad things might get, if happiness and contentment are in Christ, they're available to us because Christ is with us. Look to Christ and his solid friendship instead of waiting for circumstances to go your way.

Taking God with Us

Today, no matter what comes at you, no matter the circumstance, find contentment in Christ. Enjoy your friendship with God, and be grateful that such a valuable gift is always available.

1. What differences in you do you think there would be if you were really content, satisfied?
2. Make a mental note of circumstances that could drag you down and into a bad mood today.

3. Make a mental note of good circumstances that could give you a good day.
4. Whisper a thank-you to God for every circumstance—good and bad. See if you can rely more on your friendship with God than you do on circumstances around you today.

Parting Prayer

Father, you are so good to us. We're sorry we let circumstances get in the way and put us in a bad mood. Please change our attitude. Make us grateful. Make us content. Point out to us today each time we drift "under the circumstances."

Reporting on Contentment in Christ

Give each family member an opportunity to report honestly on the circumstances of the day and their reactions to them. Try not to judge each other's answers, but work together to grow in contentment.

1. What would make it easy for you to be content in life? Are you sure?
2. Share any curves you were thrown today, any not-so-good circumstances. Did your mood change?
3. List the good things that happened today, the good circumstances you found yourself in. Did your mood change when good things happened?
4. Were you able to get joy and contentment from your relationship with God today? Was it easier in the good or the bad circumstances?

But godliness with contentment is great gain. . . . But if we have food and clothing, we will be content with that.

—I Timothy 6:6–8

✳ Day 4 ✳

When I get to heaven, I'm going to get God to tell me about creating the funniest creations like anteaters and penguins and platypuses and maybe my friend's Uncle Jimmy. And then we'll laugh our heads off!

Dixon, 8

THE SMILE CHOICE

Did you know that it takes forty to fifty muscles to frown and only about fifteen muscles to smile? If for no other reason than to fight wrinkles, we should smile more.

Smiling is just a step away from good, healthy laughter. People the world over believe that laughter is the best medicine.

There are Institutes of Humor, as well as International Laugh Clubs, where people show up with the express purpose of laughing. Laughter has been called internal jogging. It's an exercise for the mind and the body.

It has been estimated that young children laugh an average of four hundred times a day. Grown-ups laugh an average of fifteen times a day. Somewhere along the way, we're losing hundreds of laughs.

What God Says

Shout for joy to the Lord, all the earth. Serve the Lord with gladness.

—Psalm 100:1–2

The Big Idea

What does it take to make you smile, laugh, giggle, chuckle, snicker, guffaw? Some people like pie-in-the-face humor, slapstick comedy. In the sixteenth century, Harlequin, the comic hero of Italian farce, invented a prop made of two pieces of wood joined together to make a slapping sound when he whacked the rumps of artless stooges. People dubbed his invention a slapping stick.

Others appreciate quieter, more subtle humor, a dry wit or funny jokes. But day-to-day, what touches you? Can you laugh, or at least smile, over little things?

Read through the beatitudes in Matthew 5, where Jesus begins each sentence with, "Blessed are. . . . " *Blessed* might as well read *happy.* We have to have some expression on our face all day long; it might as well be a smile.

We need to be careful not to laugh at others, to get our laughs at someone else's expense. We don't need cheap laughs. Real joy—lightheartedness—comes from inside. If we believe in Christ, then God's spirit lives in us. We're spending eternity with God. We have everything in the world to smile about!

Laughter and smiles are gifts. Use them wisely and freely.

Taking God with Us

Today, no matter what happens, smile, laugh, be happy.

1. Keep track of things that make you laugh today. Why do you think you laughed?
2. Smile at five people you've never consciously smiled at before.
3. Run an experiment to see if laughter is contagious. Can you get anyone else to laugh with you? To smile back at you?
4. Whenever you think of God today, smile and remember how blessed you are. Think of the good things in store for you.

Parting Prayer

God, remind us to smile and laugh today. Thanks for letting your spirit live in us. Help us think of you and feel grateful for the gifts you've heaped on us. Make us joyful, smiling people who reflect your Spirit.

Reporting on Joy

Give each family member an opportunity to report on smiles and laughter. If you have time and know a good joke, tell it.

1. How many times do you think you laughed today? Name a couple of specific things that made you laugh.
2. Who did you single out to receive your gift of a smile today?
3. Did you get anyone to return your smile? How did it feel when your smile was—or wasn't—returned?
4. Begin a list of all the things that you have to smile about.

Rejoice in the Lord always. I will say it again: Rejoice!

—Philippians 4:4

Day 5

I'm wondering if we all get exactly the same kind of house in heaven, no matter if you are rich or poor or just minimum wage because you don't get to take your allowance with you.

Becca, 11

MONEY, MONEY, MONEY!

Got your attention? Money gets most people's attention. But few of us know what to do with money once we get it. Ella Wendel of New York, for example, was rich by anyone's standards. But she couldn't take her millions with her when she died in 1931. So in her last will and testament, she left $30 million to Toby, her pet poodle.

More recently, in 1990, in Iowa City, Iowa, a hog named Mr. Pig and a German Shepherd dog known as Calamity Bob inherited over half a million dollars. They couldn't take it with them either.

What God Says

For we have brought nothing into the world, and we can take nothing out of it.

—I Timothy 6:7

The Big Idea

It takes money to live. Jesus worked as a carpenter. The Apostle Paul often had to ply his trade, tent making, as he traveled around preaching the Good News. Many of Jesus' original disciples were fishermen. They didn't fish for fun and relaxation but for money to live. Jesus didn't tell them they shouldn't fish, but he did teach them that it was more important to fish for people, to change lives.

If we had a nickel for every time somebody cautioned us to use our money wisely, we'd be rich, right? But what does it mean to use money wisely? Try testing your money. How much of what you've bought in the past year is still around? Most of our purchases, if we haven't gotten bored with them already, will break down sooner or later. How many of our possessions will last forever? II Corinthians 4:18 divides everything into one of two categories—temporary or eternal: "For what is seen is temporary, but what is unseen is eternal."

Things you can see	*Things you can't see*
CDs, DVDs, movies, clothes, bikes	Love, kindness, generosity, faith, joy
Couches, houses, food	Hope, peace

Later, in his letter to the Corinthians, Paul tells the believers to give to people in need. "God loves a cheerful giver" (II Corinthians 9:7). Giving to people in need is one way to use money wisely. Invest in eternity, and those invisible gifts of kindness and love may come with you after all.

Taking God with Us

Think about money today, and consider how wisely you're using your money.

1. Make a list of all the things you see today that you'd love to buy. Be honest!
2. Check over the list you made of things you'd like to buy, plus things you've bought in the past six months. Imagine what each possession will look like in a year, ten years, one hundred years.
3. List things you can't see, the "eternals" of II Corinthians 4:18. Do you see any evidence of things you can't see?
4. Come up with two specific places you could spend money toward eternal things.

Parting Prayer

Father, thank you for taking such good care of us. Show us where we're failing to use, wisely, what you've given us. Teach us how to use our money to help with your eternal plans. Keep us from falling into the trap of selfishness.

Reporting on Money

Give all family members a chance to talk about how they use their money. Don't accuse each other, but ask God to help lead you into a wiser use of money. Younger kids could draw pictures of things they want and pictures of ways they could use money wisely.

1. Compare "wish lists" of things you saw today that you'd like to buy. Then

describe what those things might look like in a few years.

2. What have you spent your money on this past year (not counting groceries, and so on)? On a scale of 1 to 10 (with 10 being perfectly wise and 1 being stupid), how wise were your purchases?
3. See how many eternal things you can come up with—things that can't be seen and won't decay.
4. Think of a few specific ways you could spend some of your money on things that don't wear out—the unseen and eternal.

Come, all you who are thirsty, come to the waters; and you who have no money, come, buy and eat! Come, buy wine and milk without money and without cost. Why spend money on what is not bread, and your labor on what does not satisfy? Listen, listen to me, and eat what is good, and your soul will delight in the richest of fare.

—Isaiah 55:1–2

Day 6

I'll tell you the difference between bad and good. When you do one, you get in big trouble. And when you do the other one, nobody notices.

Kim, 7

DO-GOODER

Andrew Carnegie and oil tycoon John D. Rockefeller were rival philanthropists, each always trying to outdo the other by giving away more money or gaining more recognition for doing good. Newspapers of the day followed the race, keeping score in a box, like sports box scores today.

In 1889, Carnegie came out with his list of what he considered the top places to give money and do good:

Universities
Hospitals
Parks
Concert halls
Swimming baths
Church buildings

The newspaper that ran Carnegie's do-gooder list received scores of angry letters to the editors, most of them from pastors who didn't like churches listed below swimming pools.

What God Says

For we are God's workmanship, created in Christ Jesus to do good works, which God prepared in advance for us to do.

—Ephesians 2:10

The Big Idea

Has anyone ever called you a do-gooder or a goodie-goodie? Chances are, they weren't paying you a compliment. So, when did it become a bad thing to be a do-gooder?

A wealthy man in California quits his job and spends his savings to start a mission to the poor. In the Midwest, a man is laid off from his job of twenty years. The next day, he learns of a family who has lost their home in a fire. He gives everything in his savings to help them. An Ohio farmer's wife saves enough money to purchase dozens of gifts for children whose parents are in prison. A man in the South spends his free time coaching Special Olympics. A woman drives her neighbor in for cancer treatments every day, even though they had never been friendly before. And none of these events make headlines.

Jesus encouraged his disciples to do good deeds, but he added that they should do their good deeds in secret, unlike the religious leaders of the day, who did all their deeds in order to be seen by others.

Ephesians 2:10 says we were created to do good works that God set up in advance. We should be on the lookout for those good deeds every day of our lives. So don't be afraid to be a do-gooder. Check your motives. Do all that you can do in secret. And look for those good deeds.

Taking God with Us

Today, go on a good-deed hunt. See if you can spot any of those good works God has waiting for you.

1. Try to notice the little nice things people do for each other—hold open a door, let someone go first, pick up a dropped pencil.
2. Do three good deeds (let someone go ahead of you or something similar). What kind of reaction do you expect to get?

3. Do one invisible good deed. If you get caught doing it, it doesn't count. Secret!
4. Prayerfully ask God during the day to show you something that needs to be done. Then ask for God's strength to help you do it.

Parting Prayer

God, thank you for giving us the perfect example of doing good. Thanks for giving us the power through Christ to do good deeds. Help us to be your servants. Guide us to those jobs you've set out and prepared for us already.

Reporting on Good Deeds

Give each family member an opportunity to contribute to the good-deed report. Pick someone to record some of the answers. Or let all family members write down or draw whatever they want.

1. Any eyewitness reports on good deeds? Were you on the receiving end of any?
2. Share family good deeds—things you've done for each other or for others. Share good deeds others have done for you.
3. Report on any good deeds you did today (but don't tell the secret good deed—that one's between you and God). Discuss how you know if you're doing good deeds from the right motive.
4. Prayerfully plan one good deed (a secret one) that you can do as a family.

Let us not become weary in doing good, for at the proper time we will reap a harvest if we do not give up. Therefore, as we have opportunity, let us do good to all people, especially to those who belong to the family of believers.

—Galatians 6:9–10

Day 7

I wonder if God gets any sleep, and if he doesn't, doesn't he ever get to dream?

Abigail, 4

DREAM ON!

Scientists claim everyone dreams at night. Even people who don't believe they dream have been shown in laboratory tests that they do dream; they just forget their dreams. We dream while we're awake, too, imagining what we could do, the places we could go, the people we might become.

Some dreams, however, make more sense than others. Arulanantham Suresh Joachim dreamed of getting into the *Guinness Book of World Records.* So he hopped an escalator in the Westfield Shopping Centre in Burwood, Australia, and traveled up and down—for 145 hours and 57 minutes, a distance of 140 miles. Lisa Burke rode an exercise bike for 42 hours and 15 minutes at a health club in Bedfordview, South Africa. They both ended up traveling nowhere. It's not enough to dream. We need the right dreams.

What God Says

For I know the plans I have for you . . . plans to prosper you and not to harm you, plans to give you hope and a future.

—Jeremiah 29:11

The Big Idea

The dictionary definitions of *dream* and *vision* have a lot in common: they refer to the art of seeing, imagining, aspiring, longing for something.

Do you know what your dreams are? Are you reaching for something that your heart tells you is for you? If you don't know where you want to end up, you'll never get there. Daydreaming isn't such a bad thing either—unless you're supposed to be listening or doing something else.

Bring God in on your dreams. If you're walking with God, talking to God, allowing Christ to live through you, you'll want the things God wants for you. Dream with God. God could zap you and make his will happen to you instantly. But he chooses to dream with you: "For I know the plans I have for you . . . to give you hope and a future."

Dream with God. With God on your side, the sky's not even the limit.

Taking God with Us

Today, dream with God. Let God in on your biggest and best dreams. Allow God to show you the plans he has for you.

1. Talk to God during the day and admit your wildest, biggest dreams.
2. Ask a friend to share his or her dreams (or just ask what your friend wants to do in the future).
3. What dreams did you used to have that you don't have any longer. Why?
4. Think about what it will take to get where you really want to be in life. Talk to God about any fears.

Parting Prayer

Father, we're excited about becoming the people you want us to be. Make us turn to you honestly and admit our deepest desires. Help us to catch your vision, to share your dreams and plans for us. We need you to guide us to the dream.

Reporting on Dreams

Give family members an opportunity to share even their wildest dreams (without making fun). Record dreams and goals so you can come back to them later.

1. What were your earliest dreams? When you were a really little kid, what did you want to be when you grew up?
2. What dreams have you already realized?
3. Share your biggest dreams, including any fears or doubts you have about achieving them.
4. Pick one family dream, something you'd like to see happen in your family. Describe in detail what the fulfillment of the dream will look like. Pray about the

dream, and plan how you can all help get there.

Therefore I do not run like a man running aimlessly.

—I Corinthians 9:26

Day 8

God talks to you way down deep in the bottom backside of your head. So when other people scream at you in the front of your head, you can't hardly hear God.

Katy, 9

PEOPLE PLEASING

Being popular—becoming a hit with people—is no guarantee that the people-pleaser pleases God. In the mid-1800s, one handsome actor was considered the greatest matinee idol of his day. Thousands of theatergoers loved him. Women adored him, sending him as many as one hundred letters each week.

Because of his popularity on- and offstage, the actor was allowed to wander backstage for the performance of "Our American Cousin" in the Ford Theater, where he assassinated President Abraham Lincoln.

The popular young actor was John Wilkes Booth.

What God Says

Am I now trying to win the approval of men, or of God? Or am I trying to please men? If I were still trying to please men, I would not be a servant of Christ.

—Galatians 1:10

The Big Idea

Be honest. Do you ever wish you were more popular? When you were deciding what to wear this morning, what was on your mind? Did you consider what people might think at school or work? Before you speak up in class or around friends, do you take into account what the others might think about what you're saying? After you've had your say, do you wonder what they thought? Why does it matter so much? Why do we waste so much time worrying about what other people think?

Trying to be popular, to please people, isn't just a waste of energy; Proverbs 29:25 warns that it's a trap. A lot of bad decisions have been made just to impress or please friends. Surveys list peer pressure as the number-one reason teens begin smoking, drinking, and taking drugs.

Even if you do please people one day, people are fickle. They change their minds. In Acts 14, Paul and Barnabas visit the city of Lystra and are a big hit when Paul heals a man who has been lame from birth. The crowd cheers. They want to worship Paul and Barnabas as gods and offer sacrifices to them. Then a couple of guys from Antioch show up and turn the crowd against Paul and Barnabas so that the people stone Paul and drag him outside the city, thinking he's dead.

People are fickle. God is not. Instead of worrying about what pleases other people, find out what pleases God. Listen to God way down deep in the bottom backside of your head.

Taking God with Us

Today, be honest with yourself and try to discover if you're a people-pleaser.

1. Throughout the day, notice when people do and say things to please other people.
2. Catch yourself worrying about what other people are thinking about you. Do you make any decisions based at least in part on what other people might think?
3. Name one thing you might have done today that you know would have pleased God but wouldn't have gone over so well with your friends.

4. Try to go against the urge to be popular today. Pick one action or say one thing that a truly popular person wouldn't do or say. Make sure it's something that pleases God (examples: sit by someone not considered "cool"; talk to and draw out someone not in the popular group).

Parting Prayer

Father, we admit that it's not easy for us to go against the crowd, especially the popular crowd. We're going to need you to change us here. Make us aware of what we're doing when we try to please people. We want to please you.

Reporting on People Pleasing

Give each family member an opportunity to report on observations from the day. Be sure each person is free to make any admissions honestly, without being judged or criticized.

1. What evidence did you see today that people are trying to be popular? Be specific.
2. Did you catch yourself trying to impress anyone today? What decisions did you make based on what your peers might think of you?
3. Is there anything you might have done differently today if your only concern had been pleasing God and not other people?
4. Were you able to pull off one activity strictly to please God? What could you do tomorrow?

Find out what pleases the Lord.

—Ephesians 5:10

Day 9

If you want to talk to God, you just say, "Thank you, God, for something to eat. Thank you, God, for something sweet." But don't say it with your mouth full.

Kayla, 8

HAPPY THANKSGIVING!

It may not be anywhere near the official Thanksgiving Day at your house, but giving thanks should be a part of every day.

Most of us know at least some version of the first Thanksgiving feast in 1621, when Pilgrims and Native Americans celebrated together. Thanksgiving didn't become official until 1863, after Sarah Josepha Hale, the first female editor of an American magazine, wrote President Lincoln, asking to set aside the last Thursday in November "as a day for national Thanksgiving and prayer."

While we're on the subject, you might as well be armed with a bit of turkey trivia. Ben Franklin believed turkeys were so much a part of America that he lobbied to have the turkey, rather than the eagle, for our national symbol. About 45 million turkeys are cooked each Thanksgiving Day, with approximately 525 million pounds of turkey eaten. (And does anybody know what you call that fleshy, dangling part that hangs from the turkey's beak in front of the throat? Some say it's a wattle. Some call it a snood.)

What God Says

Speak to one another with psalms, hymns and spiritual songs. Sing and make music in your heart to the Lord, always giving thanks to God the Father for everything, in the name of our Lord Jesus Christ.

—Ephesians 5:19–20

The Big Idea

Thanking God should be the easiest assignment we ever get. When we stop to think about all the blessings we have, it's not hard to come up with things to be thankful for. Maybe that's one reason designating one day a year as Thanksgiving is a good idea. We make ourselves stop and take an inventory of our blessings.

But those gifts and blessings are everywhere every day of the year. When's the last time you were thankful for electricity? Probably the last time a storm knocked out your power lines, right? The last time you felt wholeheartedly thankful for a cold glass of water may have been the last hot day when you were desperately thirsty.

Because we get so caught up in the rush and busyness of life, we can whirl right by incredible God-gifts without even noticing them. Taking the time to notice and to thank God through the day will not just be doing God a favor. We're the ones who will get the most out of the deal.

Taking God with Us

Today, while you're doing all the busy things you normally do—work, school, errands—pay attention. Notice God's gifts all around you. Think about all you have to be thankful for.

1. Moment-by-moment today, keep a mental note of the people and circumstances you're thankful for. Talk to God about all of them.
2. Today, notice five little things you've never thanked God for (examples: the sound of someone's voice, the way it feels when you run hard, music, sunlight).
3. Thank God sincerely for two people you've never given thanks for before today.

4. Thank God for something you don't actually feel thankful for. Trust God that he knows more about the situation than you do.

Parting Prayer

Father, we're sorry that most of the time we're so ungrateful. We forget to notice, to talk to you, to appreciate the gifts you pile around us every day. Help us to notice today, to pay attention. Thank you, thank you, thank you!

Reporting on Thanksgiving

Give each family member an opportunity to contribute to the family's thanksgiving report. It might be a good idea to keep an ongoing list of blessings and things to be thankful for. You could even pull it out on the official Thanksgiving Day.

1. Compare lists of people and circumstances you're thankful for today.

2. What little things did you notice and give thanks for today? Why do you think you never noticed those blessings before?

3. Conduct a family "thanksgiving challenge." See if you can stump each other. Think of one thing your family should be thankful for—a blessing you don't think anyone else will come up with.

4. What did you have to thank God for by faith today, without really feeling thankful? Talk about the relationship between feelings and giving thanks. Do you have to *feel* thankful to say thanks?

Be joyful always; pray continually; give thanks in all circumstances, for this is God's will for you in Christ Jesus.

—I Thessalonians 5:16–18

Day 10

Bad is when you beat somebody up and then run away. If you're good, you don't run.

—Matthew, 8

FORGIVENESS AND FRESH STARTS

Guilt can drive people to extremes. Salomea Wolf, a Spanish woman living in the early 1900s, was overwhelmed with guilt because she believed she had nagged her husband to death. In a vain attempt to make up for it, she had the portrait of her husband tattooed on her tongue. In India, a man named Gyuri tried to do penance by sticking his iron staff into a fire and licking the glowing, hot tip with his tongue. He did this five times a day for fifty-two years.

In the Middle Ages, guilt was often determined by ordeals, or tests. If the accused gave in during the ordeal, his guilt was considered proven. In a trial by water, the suspected guilty party was thrown, hands and feet bound, into the river. If he sank, he was innocent. But if he floated, he was guilty. To us, the verdicts seem turned around. But water was a symbol of purity in the medieval world. People believed that those who floated were being rejected by the water. If the water didn't reject the person, he would sink into it—innocent and free from guilt (also dead from drowning).

What God Says

As far as the east is from the west, so far has he removed our transgressions from us.

—Psalm 103:12

The Big Idea

Most of us feel guilty because we *are* guilty. We fall short of God's standard for us, sinning in acts and thoughts every day. But even though we are guilty before God, we don't have to stay that way. God offers us forgiveness because Christ has already paid for our sins. We can confess our sins to God and experience forgiveness.

Confession means agreeing with God that what we did or thought is wrong—a sin. Confession is like exhaling, getting the impurities out. But after we exhale, we need to inhale clean, fresh air to fill our lungs. Spiritually, we inhale by asking God to fill us with his Spirit. We get a fresh start—a clean slate when we ask for forgiveness.

Some people think forgiveness is just too easy. We sin, say we're sorry, and try not to do it again, and God forgives us. If that sounds easy, remember what Christ had to go through so that we could be forgiven.

He was beaten, whipped, spat on, crucified. The price of forgiveness was high. And Jesus was the only one who could pay it.

God's forgiveness is complete, not because we earn forgiveness (we can't earn it) but because Christ's death paid for our sins. In Jesus' day, the criminal's crimes were listed on a placard—a certificate of debt—and the list was posted outside the jail cell. Colossians 2 (13–14) says Christ's death canceled out our certificate of debt, marked it paid in full.

Practice spiritual breathing: exhale the sin; inhale forgiveness.

Taking God with Us

Today, practice spiritual breathing. Think about Christ and the forgiveness he earned for us.

1. Practice on-the-spot confession, admitting every bad thought or action to God.

Be sure to thank God for his on-the-spot forgiveness.

2. Pick one attitude that you know needs work (examples: you worry too much, goof off too often, think or say unkind things, care too much about what people think). Talk to God about changing your attitude.
3. Imagine what would show up on your own, personal certificate of debt nailed outside your cell.
4. Remind yourself at least five times today to thank Jesus for dying for your sins.

Parting Prayer

We know that nothing we might do could make up for the things we do wrong. Father, thank you for sending your Son to die on the cross for our sins and pay the price we couldn't. We're sorry we take that for granted so often. Remind us today of the cost of forgiveness. Teach us to breathe spiritually.

Reporting on God's Fresh Starts

Give each family member an opportunity to report on forgiveness experiences. Explore together what it means to have a fresh start.

1. How does Christ's death pay our debt for something we did today?
2. Share what you've come up with for your certificates of debt.
3. Make up a family "certificate of debt." Include sins of omission (things you should have done but didn't).
4. What can you do to show God how grateful you are for forgiveness?

Blessed is he whose transgressions are forgiven, whose sins are covered.

—Psalm 32:1–2

Day 11

God loved us even before he made us.
But he had to make us to prove it.
Patrick, 8

GOD HUGS

According to an ancient, anonymous proverb, humans need four hugs a day for survival, eight for maintenance, and twelve for growth. Hugs come in a variety of forms. Some of the classics are

- Bear hug: a solid, extended squeeze (be careful)

- Aunt hug: basically from the shoulders and above only
- Atta-Boy hug: possibly a one-sided, one-armed squeeze
- Insider hug: one hugger's hug covering another
- Private hug: for an extremely select pair (ask your parents for details)

The world's biggest hug occurred in New York City on December 1, 2000, and involved 899 bankers and carried the slogan, "One Team, One Hug."

What God Says

Praise be to the God and Father of our Lord Jesus Christ, the Father of compassion and the God of all comfort, who comforts us in all our troubles, so that we can comfort those in any trouble with the comfort we ourselves have received from God.

—II Corinthians 1:3–4

The Big Idea

Near the end of his life, as he journeyed toward Jerusalem to face crucifixion and death, Jesus cried, "O Jerusalem, Jerusalem. . . . How often I wanted to gather your children together, just as a hen gathers her brood under her wings, and you would not have it!" (Luke 13:34). Jesus wanted to hug them! He wanted to give them his comfort.

One of the things the Apostle Paul prayed for the new believers—one of the most frequent prayer requests that turn up in his letters to the churches—was that they could sense and know Christ's comfort and love. No matter what kind of persecutions they were going through, Paul assured them that Jesus had gone there first and was right there with them to help them get through it, too. Jesus could comfort because he had lived in human skin and understood what they were going through.

No matter where your day takes you today, no matter what happens, you can turn to God for comfort. Get a spiritual hug from the Creator of arms and hearts and hugs.

God gives the best hugs!

Taking God with Us

Today, as you move from place to place, keep in mind that God is right there with you, walking through everything you are.

1. Before you arrive at school or work, or begin your routine day, close your eyes and imagine climbing onto God's lap and getting a bear hug.
2. Be on the lookout for hugs today. Try to guess the purpose and the effect of the hugs.
3. When something good happens, imagine sharing a hug with God. Let God in on it.

4. If something hurts or disappoints you today, ask God for comfort and thank God that he's always there to comfort you.

Parting Prayer

Father, thank you for sending your Son to walk around the way we do and experience the things that hurt and disappoint us. Thanks for understanding. We need your comfort and compassion. We need your hugs. Remind us to ask for them. Amen.

Reporting on God Hugs

Give each family member an opportunity to make a "hug report." One person might record all the responses. Someone else might draw a picture.

1. Make up your own list of hugs and their definitions.
2. Did anyone observe any hugs today? What kind of hugs were they? Could you guess the reasons for and the effects of the hugs?
3. Did you ask for a God hug today? What happened?
4. Try a family group hug. You could come up with a secret password to usher in a family hug whenever you feel the need.

When anxiety was great within me, your consolation brought joy to my soul.

—Psalm 94:19

Day 12

It takes four years to get your prayer answered. I know because I asked for a puppy when I was three, and I just got one.

Carlo, 7

WAITING ON GOD

When most of us pray to God, we'd love to get instant answers: deposit the prayer, and take out the answer from the prayer-vending machine. But prayer rarely works that way, and we end up waiting on God. People who have spent time in God's waiting room can come up with all kinds of theories on why God makes us wait. Here are some ideas from kids:

God takes only one day to answer your prayer in the summer, and eight days to answer in the winter. Only he takes forever if you're asking for a Barbie doll. —Angela, 6

Sometimes when you ask God something, he doesn't answer right away because he knows you're only going to change your mind soon as he does it.—Carson, 7

Sometimes you think you're waiting, but he's done and he's done said no. —Missy, 7

When you ask God something, he don't like to do it right away for some reason—that's his own business. But if you wait, he'll get there. He'll get there.—Byron, 8

What God Says

I wait for the Lord, my soul waits, and in his word I put my hope. My soul waits for the Lord more than watchmen wait for the morning, more than watchmen wait for the morning.

—Psalm 130:5–6

The Big Idea

God doesn't always say yes to our prayers—or no. He sometimes says wait. And for many of us, that's the hardest answer to get. All through the Bible, God made people wait. Some, like Sarah, Hannah, and Elizabeth, waited and prayed for a baby until they were too old to have one. Then God gave them children.

Others, like David, found out God's will for them. But they had to wait years before that will was realized. David was anointed King of Israel in I Samuel 16:13, but he didn't get to begin his reign until II Samuel 5. In the meantime, he had to go back to herding his father's sheep and, later, playing the harp for cranky King Saul. God used the waiting time to develop character. Sarah, Hannah,

Elizabeth, and David became better people, closer to God because of the time logged with him in the waiting room.

When God makes you wait for an answer to your prayer, remember that you're not alone in that waiting room. Talk to God about it. Scooch closer to him. And trust. The psalmist encourages us to wait like "watchmen for the morning." Watchmen waited with total faith; they knew morning would come. That's the kind of faith that comes with waiting.

Taking God with Us

Today, while you're doing all the busy things you normally do, keep in mind the things you're waiting for.

1. Every time you sit down today, imagine yourself in a waiting room, waiting with God. Chat with God about things you're waiting for.

2. Try to remember any "no" answers you've received to past prayers. Remember the "yes" answers, too!
3. Try imagining what your life would have been like if God had answered all of your prayers with an instant yes.
4. Pray for at least one new thing today, asking God for something that you think is in God's will for you.

Parting Prayer

God, thanks for caring about the people we're becoming. Thanks for always being beside us while we're in the waiting room. Help us to trust you, to trust your answers and your timing. Remind us today of how faithful you've been in the past answering our prayers. Amen.

Reporting on God's Waiting Room

Give each family member an opportunity to report on past and present prayers. You might want to keep a list of "wait" answers and fill in the outcome later.

1. Share specific "yes" answers received to prayers in the past.
2. Share prayers that God has answered no to. Can you understand any more clearly now why God may have answered no? (We can't always see why, even in retrospect.)
3. What are some major things you've had to wait on God for? How did the waiting affect you?
4. What things are you waiting on now?

But if we hope for what we do not yet have we wait for it patiently.

—Romans 8:25

Day 13

Sometimes you just gotta do what you gotta do. Jesus may have been God's only son, but he still had to go to school.

Stephen, 7

SALT of THE EARTH

You may not think much about salt. Most food has so much salt in it, you might not even use that salt shaker often. But in biblical times, salt was so valuable that some cultures used it as money. In fact, the words *salt* and *salary* have a similar derivation. And good people have long been described as the "salt of the earth"; they did what had to be done.

Salt was an integral part of society. People couldn't survive without salt in the diet; they needed it to retain water. Newborn babies were rubbed with salt. If you had a toothache, you'd be told to put a grain of salt in the cavity. Since there were no fridges, meat and fish were packed in salt to preserve them. Eventually, salt was used to tan leather and make glass. Salt was even a part of worship. All temple sacrifices had to be salted first.

We still need salt. As a seasoning, salt flavors any food it's added to. Where would we be without salt? Without it, saltwater taffy would just be water taffy. And popcorn wouldn't even taste like popcorn!

What God Says

You are the salt of the earth. But if the salt loses its saltiness, how can it be made salty again? It is no longer good for anything, except to be thrown out and trampled by men.

—Matthew 5:13

The Big Idea

Imagine that your school or workplace or neighborhood put you on trial for being different. They want to convict you of being a Christian. The prosecution calls as its first witness, your teacher (or your boss).

"Please tell us how the accused stands out as a Christian. Is there an unusual degree of honesty and kindness? Does this Christian always work hard, without complaining?"

The next witness is brought out—your best friend. "Tell us, please, how this Christian has refused to take part in gossip and complaining. What actions and attitudes have branded this person as different, living by a separate code of life? And how exactly has this Christian's influence changed—flavored—your group of friends?"

For the last witness, the prosecution calls your enemy—the one person you have the most trouble getting along with—and says, "Will you please give us proof that this Christian treats you differently than your other enemies treat you?"

And after friends and enemies, acquaintances and family have testified, will there be enough evidence to convict you of being different? Of flavoring like salt? Of being a Christian? Or has your salt lost its flavor?

Taking God with Us

Today, with whatever group you find yourself, think of yourself as salt, even possibly as salt of the earth.

1. In what way do you blend in with other people at school or work or in the neighborhood?
2. In what ways do you stand out, different because of your faith in Christ?
3. Observe how others affect a group when they join it. How do you affect a group?

4. Pick one time, one conversation today and imagine yourself as salt. See if you can change the direction and spirit of a group.

Parting Prayer

Father, thank you for all you've done for us to make us different, forgiven, and yours. Help us to be grateful enough to belong to you that we're not ashamed to be different. Show us ways we've lost our saltiness, and make us salty again.

Reporting on Saltiness

Give each family member an opportunity to report on the salt level in your family.

1. If your family were put on trial for being Christian, what evidence would there be to convict? Make a list.

2. Describe one experience, one incident when you know you seasoned a group, changing the attitude or actions of other people.
3. How would your day or week have looked if you'd been saltier?
4. Why do you think we don't want to stand out in our crowds?

Let your conversation be always full of grace, seasoned with salt, so that you may know how to answer everyone.

—Colossians 4:6

Day 14

The devil is a big temptation bug! He whispers in your ear, "I know your mama said don't play in the street, but go get your skateboard. That street sure looks good to me."

–Dajuan, 10

YOU CAN'T MAKE ME!

Temptation is all around us, as near as the closest french fry. According to a group of American researchers, Americans spend $50 billion a year on diet-related products (and still we're overweight). At any given time, 45 percent of women and 25 percent of men are on a diet. We follow no-protein diets and all-protein diets; we eat no carbohydrates or we're carbohydrate-loading; we're fasting or eating nine meals a day.

One dieter, Nick Russo of Miami, Florida, had given into temptation so many times that in 1989 he placed posters in his favorite restaurants offering a reward of $25,000 to anyone who caught him eating.

There has to be a better way to keep us from temptation!

What God Says

No temptation has seized you except what is common to man. And God is faithful; he will not let you to be tempted beyond what you can bear. But when you are tempted, he will also provide a way out so that you can stand up under it.

—I Corinthians 10:13–14

The Big Idea

Self-control is underrated! If you could keep yourself from doing things you'll regret, and if you could discipline yourself to do the things you need and want to do in life, most of your battles would be won. In fact, they might not even be waged. We should all be standing in line, piggy banks in hand, ready to do whatever it takes to get self-control.

God never said we wouldn't be tempted. Instead, we get reminded that Jesus was tempted just as we are, but he didn't give in to temptation. And we get the promise that he'll show us the way to escape. No matter how strong the temptation, Christ in us is stronger.

So, how do we escape temptation? Paul gives Timothy some good ideas in II Timothy 2:22: "Flee the evil desires of youth, and pursue righteousness, faith, love and peace, along with those who call on the Lord out of a pure heart." Part one of Paul's advice is, "Run away!" Sometimes the best way to stay out of trouble is to run away from it. Part Two is, "Run toward!" Do whatever you can to catch hold of righteousness, faith, love, and peace with friends who love God as you do. If we're walking in the right direction, we'll steer clear of some of the traps wait-ing off the path. And if we're in hot pursuit of goodness, we'll race by without even seeing a lot of the temptations.

Taking God with Us

Today, keep track of the temptations all around you and how you handle them.

1. What do you think are the major temptations you face every day? Include thoughts, attitudes, things you do, and things you don't do.
2. What's your biggest temptation? Is it possible to run away from it?
3. Are the people you spend time with "friends who call on the Lord out of a pure heart"? What do you think that means?
4. What could you do today to run toward righteousness and faith and love? Be specific. What could you do differently?

Parting Prayer

God, thank you for becoming like us and letting yourself be tempted the way we are. We know that you understand how we feel. Help us to look to you for help when we're tempted. Help us to follow you and draw closer to you every day so we'll be prepared to say no when we need to and yes when you want us to.

Reporting on Temptations

Give each family member an opportunity to report honestly on temptations. If someone records the temptations, the list might be helpful for future prayer requests.

1. What do you think the difference is between temptation and sin? Come up with specific examples and see if you agree.

2. What temptations did you run across today? How did you handle them?
3. Give examples of temptations you've chosen to run away from. Where have you been able to exercise good self-control?
4. What could you do to chase after righteousness and faith and love? Is there any way you can help each other as a family?

When tempted, no one should say, "God is tempting me." For God cannot be tempted by evil, nor does he tempt anyone; but each one is tempted when, by his own evil desire, he is dragged away and enticed.

—James 1:13–14

Day 15

okay. I admit I'm afraid of snakes but only their heads and tails. Does that count?

Chad, 9

GOD ROCKS

People are afraid of many different things. King Henry III of France, Louis XIV of France, and Napoleon all suffered from ailurophobia—a fear of cats. Other fears named and classified are

Ablutophobia—fear of washing
Acarophobia—fear of itching

Achluophobia or myctophobia—fear of darkness
Acrophobia—fear of heights
Acousticophobia—fear of noise
Ligyrophobia—fear of loud noises
Arrhenphobia or hominophobia—fear of men
Cathisophobia—fear of sitting
Bufonophobia—fear of toads
Ranidapphobia—fear of frogs
Blennophobia or myxophobia—fear of slime
Lutraphobia—fear of otters
Chaetophobia—fear of hair
Peladophobia—fear of bald people
Motorphobia—fear of automobiles
Papyrophobia—fear of paper
Melissophobia—fear of bees
Hypnophobia or somniphobia—fear of sleep
Porphyrophobia—fear of the color purple
Philophobia—fear of falling in love

What God Says

For in the day of trouble, he will keep me safe in his dwelling; he will hide me in the shelter of his tabernacle and set me high upon a rock.

—Psalm 27:5

The Big Idea

Most of us would like a guarantee that we'll be safe and that the world's troubles won't reach us. The insurance business is a testimony to that fact. A London insurance company, Goodfellows, sold 40,000 "Alien All Risks" policies, guaranteeing payment of $1.7 million in case of alien abduction or impregnation.

One insurance company rose to fame with the slogan, "Get a piece of the rock." But there's only one Rock—God. The Psalms are filled with cries to "the Rock of our salvation" and "my Rock and refuge."

Although God never promised a trouble-free life, he did promise to be right there with a refuge—a place of escape and safety. Throughout history, people have hidden in churches, cathedrals, and synagogues and claimed sanctuary—safety. Because Jesus lives in us, that safe place, the refuge from trouble, is even nearer than the nearest church.

Imagine running into a warm barn to get out of a thunderstorm or dashing to the fireside of a cozy inn to get out of a blizzard. Now picture climbing up onto God's lap to escape whatever fear is snapping at your heels.

Taking God with Us

Today, even during the busiest times of the day, take secret time-outs and dash into God, your refuge.

1. When do you feel the need to escape to a safe place? What are some of the threats in the world that make you feel unsafe?
2. Try to remember times in your life when you've hidden from some threat. Where did you go to hide?

3. At some point during your day, escape. Imagine leaving the noise and problems and stepping into a quiet place with God. Then talk to God about your troubles.
4. Pick one fear, and talk to God about it during the day.

Parting Prayer

Father, we admit that we feel afraid sometimes. At times, we feel like running away and hiding. Help us to hide in you. Thank you for always giving us refuge—a safe place to go. Help us to run to you today, to duck into your safe house and give you our fears.

Reporting on Fears

Give each family member an opportunity to admit fears honestly. Make your family discussions safe places to talk about those fears.

1. List your Top Ten family fears.
2. How has God helped you find calm and safety in the middle of troubles and fears in the past?
3. Name one specific fear that bugged you today? How did you handle it?
4. How is God like a rock? List as many ways as you can.

The Lord is my rock, my fortress and my deliverer; my God is my rock, in whom I take refuge.

—Psalm 18:2

Day 16

Nobody cries in heaven because well, okay. Remember how great Christmas was? Well, it's Christmas every day in heaven!

Thomas, 7

BOTTLED TEARS

Humans have good reason to cry. When we get upset, our brains and bodies work overtime producing chemicals and hormones we don't need. Crying helps get rid of the extra chemicals. When we "cry our eyes out," the chemicals disappear, along with the excess hormones, as the tears flow from our eyes and down our cheeks. Getting rid of the chemical agents can help soothe distress and grief. That's why many (but not all) people feel better after a good cry.

Ever wonder why onions—innocent members of the lily family—make us cry? It's not the strong smell. It's a gas that's released from the onion when we slice it. Onions contain an oil that is part sulfur; when you cut an onion, you disturb a gas inside called propanethiol S-oxide. The gas mixes with the enzymes in the onion and gives off a passive sulfur compound. When that gas drifts up and hits the water produced by your tear ducts, voila! It produces sulfuric acid. But your tears will eventually wash it all away.

What God Says

Put my tears in Thy bottle; Are they not in Thy book?

—Psalm 56:8 NASV

The Big Idea

Crying is natural. It's part of the way our bodies work. Still, crying doesn't necessarily help us spiritually or emotionally. The prophet Hosea criticized the other prophets of his day because they cried on their beds but didn't change their ways. They cried out, but not to God. They were just railing about how tough things were for them.

On the other hand, Jesus himself cried. He didn't cry for himself but for his friends, who were grieving over the death of their brother Lazarus. Jesus knew he was about to perform his greatest miracle and bring about the resurrection of Lazarus from the dead. But he still cried over the sadness and distress of Martha and Mary.

The writer of Psalm 56 pictures God as saving tears in a bottle. We only save the things that are valuable—a clipping from a first haircut, a birth announcement, a wedding invitation. Our tears are valuable to God.

In the Sermon on the Mount, Jesus made a promise to those who mourn and weep: “Blessed are you who weep now, for you will laugh” (Luke 6:21). Our years on earth aren’t even a speck in the timeline of eternity. Go on and cry now. For the rest of eternity, better things are waiting. Jesus is waiting, too, and he promises we won’t have to cry in heaven:

He will wipe every tear from their eyes. There will be no more death or mourning or crying or pain, for the old order of things has passed away.

—Revelation 21:4

Taking God with Us

Today, pay attention to your moods. Remember the things that have made you sad—that still make you feel like crying.

1. Think about the last time you had a good cry. Did it help or not?
2. Think about the last time you felt like crying but didn't. Did you let God in on the way you felt?
3. Today, pay attention to the sadness of others. Can you tell who's feeling sad? Is there anything you could do to help?
4. Most days have ups and downs. If anything makes you down today, pay attention. Is it the kind of thing that usually makes you sad? Talk to God about it.

Parting Prayer

Father, thank you for loving us so much that you'd save our tears in a bottle. With a whole world to create and sustain, it's amazing that you care about the things that make us sad. Help us to turn to you when we feel like crying, when we do cry. And help us to care about the sadness of others today.

Reporting on Tears

Give family members an opportunity to talk about the things that make them sad. Share hope and healing together, too.

1. Share the last time you had a good cry. Did it help or not?
2. Did you observe sadness in anyone else today? Talk about ways you can help when a friend feels sad.
3. Be honest. Are you sad right now? Why? What would help?
4. God saves our tears in a bottle. Consider starting a family "tear jar." Designate a jar or a box where anyone in the family might drop in a particular sadness (drawn or written). Decide if it's OK to read from the tear jar or if it's private and for "blind" prayers only.

Weeping may remain for a night, but rejoicing comes in the morning.

—Psalm 30:5

Day 17

I would like to ask God what there is to do in heaven. And what the rules are like up there. Does he allow eating ice cream in *his* living room?

Nicky, 9

RULES, RULES, RULES

Rules and laws are everywhere. Here are just a few of the unusual laws still on the books. In some states, it's against the law to

- Drive blindfolded
- Flirt (if you're a man)
- Wear a fake mustache to church

- Throw a ball at someone's head on purpose
- Spit in front of women
- Wear slippers after 10 P.M.
- Carry an ice cream cone in your back pocket
- Jump off a building
- Flick boogers into the wind (under penalty of death)
- Howl at ladies within city limits
- Walk on the street with untied shoelaces
- Take a bite out of another's hamburger
- Walk backwards downtown while eating a hamburger
- Make "ugly faces" at dogs
- Wear boots to bed
- Put hypnotized people in display windows
- Read comics while driving
- Throw pickle juice on a trolley

What God Says

Do you want to be free from the one in authority? Then do what is right and he will commend you.

—Romans 13:3

The Big Idea

How do you feel about rules? Few of us can honestly say we love restrictions and rules. But listen to what David says about rules and laws in Psalm 119: "O how I love your law!" (v.97); "I delight in your decrees" (v.16); "My soul is consumed with longing for your laws at all times" (v.20); "Direct me in the path of your commands, for there I find delight" (v.35); "I reach out my hands for your commandments, which I love" (v.48); "Seven times a day I praise you for your righteous laws" (v.164).

Why does David love God's laws so much? Psalm 119 is filled with reasons. David says he wants to keep God's laws because then he won't be ashamed (v.6); he will have understanding (v.32) and peace (v.165). And to top it all off: "I have more insight than all my teachers" (v.99)! God doesn't just give us a bunch of rules to prove he's powerful. He created us and knows what will—and won't—work to give us the best possible life. His laws are our owners' manual.

Not all laws come directly from God (like some of the silly ones in this chapter). But we're still encouraged to obey the laws of the land so that we don't have to be afraid of authority. We obey parents (even when their rules seem silly) because it's part of honoring them.

Taking God with Us

As you go through your day today, think about all the rules in place, keeping order wherever you go.

1. List rules you follow as you go through your day (speed limits, school rules, property laws, and so on).
2. Police yourself, and see if you break or bend any rule (including house rules and God's laws). What rules are the hardest for you to follow?
3. Are there any rules you'd like to see thrown out?
4. If you could make three rules that would affect your daily life, what would they be?

Parting Prayer

God, help us delight in your law the way David did in Psalm 119. We're grateful that you've given us principles to follow so we won't wreck our own lives. Help us notice when we break one of your laws. Fill us with your love and your Spirit, and help us fulfill your laws.

Reporting on Rules

Give each family member an opportunity to report on the rules encountered during the day. You might want to start a list of house rules.

1. What rules did you follow today? Name as many of them as you can.
2. Which rules are the hardest for you to keep? Did you break any today?
3. Talk about some of God's laws and how they protect us and make us wiser and happier.
4. Are there any house rules you think should be dropped? Added? Together, imagine the changes that might occur if you did drop or add each rule.

[The laws of the Lord] are more precious than gold, than much pure gold; they are sweeter

than honey, than honey from the comb.
By them is your servant warned; in keeping
them there is great reward.

—Psalm 19:10–11

Day 18

My wish for the world is there'd be no fighting anywhere, everybody would get along, nobody would use drugs, we'd take care of the trees and air and everybody's perm would turn out nicely.

Maureen, 5

TOSS IT UP!

Worries can stick to us like sidewalk gum to a tennis shoe. People have always shown a love for sticky things. The ancient Greeks chewed mastiche in 50 A.D., and the Mayans of South America chewed chicle in 200 A.D. The first commercial gum was made and sold in 1848. But by then, Native Americans had been chewing spruce resin for years.

According to *Forbes* magazine, November 8, 1992, we chew between 150 and 200 sticks of gum per person per year. And we blow bubbles. The largest bubble on record was 23 inches in diameter (Susan Montgomery Williams, USA, 1994). The largest bubble-gum bubble blown with the nose, as opposed to the mouth, was 11 inches (Joyce Samuels, USA, 2000).

And just in case you're in a foreign country and need gum, here are a few translations:

Russian—*zhevatelnaya rezinka*
Japanese—*gamu*
Norwegian—*tyggegummi*
Swiss—*chaetschgummi*
Swedish—*tuggumi*
German—*kaugummi*

What God Says

Humble yourselves, therefore, under God's mighty hand, that he may lift you up in due time. Cast all your anxiety on him because he cares for you.

—I Peter 5:6–7

The Big Idea

Did you ever try to make taffy? Ever get gum or glue stuck on your fingers? The more you work with it, rubbing and stretching, the stickier it gets and the harder it is to throw off. Worry can be like that. God wants us to cast our worries on him, to toss them up. But we get sticky fingers and have trouble letting go.

Why is it so hard to toss up worries? Most of us try to think and rethink our concerns, mulling over the worst that could happen. We want one more try to make it go away. We might even pray and ask God to take the worry away, but we keep reworking the sticky problem, taking it back, aiming again, not quite trusting that God has it under control.

When Peter wrote the young churches and encouraged them to cast anxiety on him, he included a tip on how they could get rid of the sticky worries. Humble yourselves.

To be humble just means to have a right evaluation of yourself, to see yourself accurately, as God does. When we hang on to our worries, we're actually saying that we think we're great enough to handle them on our own. It's humbling to admit we can't. We need God to handle this one.

Peter ends with the best motivation for tossing up worries: because God cares for you. Picture God, arms outstretched, waiting to take that worry for good. Toss it up!

Taking God with Us

Today, try to catch yourself worrying. Be on guard for sticky worries.

1. Think of three worries that come up the most often in your life. How do you usually handle them?
2. The first time you catch yourself worrying today, stop! Try tossing it up to God—praying about it, then releasing it.

3. What are your friends worried about? Decide what you think they're worried about. Then ask them.
4. At the end of the day, check in with God and decide if you really did toss up your worries today or if you've taken them back.

Parting Prayer

Father, thank you for caring about us so much that you'd want to bother with our worries, even the silliest, smallest concerns. We're sorry that we keep taking them back. Help us trust you. We admit that we can't handle everything on our own. Help us to trust you. Give us your peace.

Reporting on Sticky Worries

Give each family member an opportunity to share sticky worries. You might want to make a list of the worries and check back to see if the worries have stayed in God's hands.

1. Honestly share the worries you wrestle with every day.
2. Why are these worries so sticky and hard to let go of?
3. Humble yourself. Talk about why you need God to take these worries from you—why you can't handle them on your own.
4. Pray together and toss up anxieties to God. Thank God for catching them.

My heart is not proud, O Lord, my eyes are not haughty; I do not concern myself with great matters or things too wonderful for me. But I have stilled and quieted my soul; like a weaned child with its mother, like a weaned child is my soul within me.

—Psalm 131:1–2

Day 19

Don't eat cigarettes, and don't take whiskey, and don't eat drugs and forget how to read. Oh yeah, and don't wear shorts in the winter.

Michael, 6

So WHAT WOULD JESUS DO?

In 1820, C. C. Colton, a British author and clergyman, said, "Imitation is the sincerest flattery." We learn most things, like talking and walking, by imitation.

There's even a new science founded on the principles of imitation—biomimicry. Scientists study designs found in nature, then imitate those patterns to solve problems or make designs of their own. Ceramic tiles are designed and produced imitating an abalone. One company used a leaf as a model for a solar cell to harness energy. Another company runs its business like a hickory forest.

England's King Charles II (1630–1685) wanted to be like history's powerful rulers, so he had dust collected from the Egyptian mummies. Then he rubbed mummy dust onto his skin in the belief that the greatness of the pharaohs would rub off on him. It didn't.

What God Says

Do not conform any longer to the pattern of this world, but be transformed by the renewing of your mind. Then you will be able to test and approve what God's will is—his good, pleasing and perfect will.

—Romans 12:2

The Big Idea

Imitation, or trying to conform to the actions of another person, is a natural, human response. When we envy or admire someone, why not try to do the things that person does? Because not all people and not all actions end up helping to make us the people we want to be. If we conform to the wrong crowd, we just might end up "eating cigarettes, taking whiskey, eating drugs, and forgetting how to read." We have to be confident of the person we choose to imitate.

Jesus came to earth and "lived in our skin," walked in our world, giving us a perfect example to follow, to imitate. We can read the four gospels and see Jesus in action, helping the poor, loving his enemies, obeying his Father, praying, teaching, sacrificing his life.

But Jesus offers us more help than just being a good example. Besides giving us a clear picture of what Jesus would do, God transforms us, changes us so that we're more like Jesus. Romans 12:2 says if we want to prove what God's will is, we should stop being conformed and be transformed instead. For every decision, you can choose to conform, to do what everybody else is doing, or choose to be like Jesus and live like him. Galatians 5:25 says, "Since we live by the Spirit, let us keep in step with the Spirit. Follow in his footsteps."

The disciples didn't always imitate Jesus while they were with him. But after the resurrection, they were transformed, changed. When Peter and John bravely stood up against the religious leaders and spoke to huge crowds, Acts 4:13 says the people took note that these men had been with Jesus. Jesus had rubbed off on them, and it showed.

Taking God with Us

Today, try to notice how many decisions you're making. Ask yourself what Jesus would do—then do it!

1. Keep track of things you do today that are Christlike—things you want to do naturally because God is transforming you on the inside.
2. Three times today, stop and ask yourself what Jesus would do in your situation.
3. Jesus cared for people who were left out, outcasts. At school or at work or at home, do one thing for someone who usually gets left out.
4. Philippians says that Jesus considered other people to be more important than himself. Try it one time today (let someone go first; don't grab the best; look out for someone else).

Parting Prayer

God, thanks for sending Jesus as our example, and thanks for promising to make us more like Jesus. Help us not to just do what everybody else is doing. Change us from the inside. Make us want the things you want. Make us more like Jesus today.

Reporting on What Jesus Would Do

Give each family member an opportunity to report on God's activity today. Talk about tough decisions and conforming to the crowd.

1. What did you do today that you think Jesus would have done?
2. Tell the truth. Are you doing anything (anything at all) that you doubt Jesus would have done? What can you do about it?

3. How many times did you wonder what Jesus would have done today? If you didn't, why do you think that is?

4. Name some situations when it's easy to conform, to follow the crowd instead of following Jesus.

Be imitators of God, therefore, as dearly loved children and live a life of love, just as Christ loved us and gave himself up for us as a fragrant offering and sacrifice to God.
—Ephesians 5:1–2

Day 20

When Jesus was a little boy, he went to his church and got hisself lost. It happens.

Tressa, 7

FOLLOW THE LIGHT

"Lightning bugs" or fireflies are called *cucujos* in the West Indies and South America, where they give off a glow bright enough to read by. Some people, when they travel in the dark of night and are afraid they may get lost, still place the *cucujos* in lanterns for light.

Here's how you tell a girl lightning bug from a boy lightning bug: the boys are the ones that light up the sky at night. Females respond from perches on or near the ground. But before you get any ideas about boy lightning bugs being brighter than girls, think again. If a male zooms down to the wrong girl, one out of his species, she's likely to eat him.

Some Australians still use camels to carry goods over the desert. Unfortunately, unlike lightning bugs, camels don't have their own lights. So, to avoid accidents with trucks and cars, the camel owner attaches lights to the camel's tail—"tail lights."

What God Says

Your word is a lamp to my feet and a light for my path.

—Psalm 119:105

The Big Idea

When you walk into a dark house, the first thing you do is turn on the light. That way, you won't stumble over things, and you can find your way around. Life isn't quite as scary in the day as it is at night.

Those qualities of light are part of what the psalmist means when he says that the Word is a lamp to his feet and a light to his path. The Word—the Bible—keeps us from stumbling over sin; it shows us which way to go so we won't get lost, and it keeps us from being afraid. At least 90 percent of God's will is given in the Bible—principles on how to live, how to grow spiritually, how to have a relationship with God, how to have relationships with other people. Scripture shines a light to help us get where we need to go.

But the psalmist makes it clear that we don't get a spotlight; we get a flashlight, a lamp at our feet, enough to show us the next step. And that's enough to allow God to transform us into the light. Jesus said, "You are the light of the world. . . . Let your light shine before men, that they may see your good deeds and praise your Father in heaven" (Matthew 5:14–16).

God began the world with the command, "Let there be light!" And for all eternity, God himself will be our light: "The city does not need the sun or the moon to shine on it, for the glory of God gives it light, and the Lamb is its lamp" (Revelation 21:23).

Taking God with Us

Today, pay attention to light in all its forms. Let it remind you that God gives you light and you are the light of the world.

1. Today, whenever you notice the light of the sun or moon, or when you notice an

artificial light at school or work or anywhere, think about what the light does, how it helps.

2. Come up with two ways that God and his Word are like a light that you see today.
3. Can you remember a time when the Bible helped you make a decision or solve a problem?
4. If you're wrestling with a big decision, ask God to light up the next step for you to take.

Parting Prayer

Father, thank you for being the light and for being involved in everything we do. Today, remind us that you're there, showing us every step. Help us to be the light, too. Shine through us.

Reporting on God's Light

Give each family member an opportunity to report on discoveries in light today.

1. What different kinds of light did you notice today?
2. How did light remind you of what God is like and what we should be like?
3. Talk about times when God has used his Word, the Bible, to show you his will and light up the next step to take.
4. Where do you wish God would shine a spotlight and show you the whole path instead of a flashlight for a step at a time? Why do you think we can only see a little distance ahead?

For you were once darkness, but now you are light in the Lord. Live as children of light (for the fruit of the light consists in all goodness, righteousness and truth)

—Ephesians 5:8–9

Day 21

When you get your room in heaven, you don't have to share it with any of your brothers. Or, if you do have to share, God makes you so you don't mind sharing.

Adrian, 6

SHARE AND SHARE ALIKE

A young woman in Minnesota found an old man eating out of the dumpster behind the restaurant where she worked as a waitress. Remembering teachings she had heard as a child (share and share alike; do unto others as you would have them do to you), she gave the man her sandwich. After visiting with him during her break, she invited him to come by her apartment that evening for a home-cooked meal.

That night, after they shared the food she had on hand, the woman told him that he was welcome to eat supper with her whenever he needed a meal. The man returned the next night—with a friend. From there, the suppers continued to grow and the woman continued to share. Twenty years later, she was feeding between one hundred to two hundred homeless people from her own kitchen six nights a week.

What God Says

And do not forget to do good and to share with others, for with such sacrifices God is pleased.

—Hebrews 13:16

The Big Idea

If you've spent much time with babies (little brothers and sisters count), you know that one of the first things a baby can do is grab. We're not born sharers. Learning to share is one of the first lessons children are taught—and it's rarely a welcome one.

Jesus taught that if someone wants your coat, you should give him the shirt off your back. If someone asks you to go a mile with him, go two. God makes it clear we should share—our time, our talents and gifts, our money, our stuff.

Sharing goes against our human nature. It's hard enough to share with family and friends. They might even appreciate our generosity. But we're supposed to share with everyone—even strangers, even enemies.

Jesus explained that God, the King, would greet his sharing children with open arms. "Then the King will say . . . 'Come, you who are blessed by my father. . . . For I was hungry and you gave me something to eat, I was thirsty and you gave me something to drink, I was a stranger and you invited me in, I needed clothes and you clothed me, I was sick and you looked after me, I was in prison and you came to visit me.' Then the righteous will answer him, 'Lord, when did we see you hungry and feed you, or thirsty and give you something to drink? When did we see you a stranger and invite you in, or needing clothes and clothe you? When did we see you sick or in prison and go to visit you?' The King will reply, 'I tell you the truth, whatever you did for one of the least of these brothers of mine, you did for me'" (Matthew 25:34–40).

Share for Jesus. Don't expect anything in return, except the satisfaction of knowing that you're making God happy.

Taking God with Us

Today, make it a point to take advantage of every opportunity to share.

1. How many shared things have you already taken advantage of today (household things, someone's time, help with something)?

2. During the day, come up with three things other people shared with you and three things you shared with other people.
3. Of all the things you possess, what would be the hardest for you to share with someone you're not that crazy about? Why?
4. As you go through your day, keep a mental list of sharing in action, that is, sharing you observe going on around you.

Parting Prayer

Father, thank you for loving us so much that you share your world and even eternity with us. Show us areas where we're being selfish with our time, our talents, our treasure. Help us to share the things you've given us. We know that all we have comes from you.

Reporting on Sharing

Give each family member an opportunity to report on sharing. Together, you might discuss some goals your family can share, as well as ideas for sharing what God has given you.

1. What things are the hardest for you to share with family members? Why do you think it's so hard?
2. Is it ever OK not to share? When? How do you know?
3. Take turns pointing out and thanking each other for time and stuff shared inside your family. Be specific.
4. How is your family doing in their effort to share the blessings God has given each of you? What else could you do to share with others?

Command them to do good, to be rich in good deeds, and to be generous and willing to share. In this way they will lay up treasure for themselves as a firm foundation for the coming age, so that they may take hold of the life that is truly life.

—I Timothy 6:18–19

Day 22

Angels pull people out of burning cars and out of quicksand, and keep people from being shot or falling out of airplanes, and they help you with subtraction.

Kayla, 9

HELP!

Stories abound of narrow escapes and miraculous close calls:

- In 1988, two workers in New York City's Empire State Building stepped onto one of the sixty-four elevators. The elevator cable broke, and the men fell forty stories (four hundred feet) in four seconds. The elevator then stopped near the fourth floor, and the men walked out with only minor bruises.

- In 1972, Vesna Vulovic was a flight attendant on a DC-9 airplane that blew up over Czechoslovakia and fell 33,300 feet to the ground. She survived.
- United States park ranger Roy C. Sullivan survived being struck by lightning seven times between 1942 and 1977. This "human lightning conductor" had his hair catch on fire, lost a toenail, singed his eyebrows, and suffered injuries to his arms, legs, stomach, and chest. But in 1983, Mr. Sullivan committed suicide after breaking up with his girlfriend.

What God Says

For he will command his angels concerning you to guard you in all your ways; they will lift you up in their hands, so that you will not strike your foot against a stone.

—Psalm 91:11–12

The Big Idea

The first description of an angel comes in Genesis 16:7 and the last in Revelation 22:16. Jesus warned people that children are protected by angels: “See that you do not look down on one of these little ones. For I tell you that their angels in heaven always see the face of my Father in heaven” (Matthew 18:10).

Angels were with Jesus in the Garden. They could have rescued him from the cross if he had chosen to call on them. And angels were in the tomb after the resurrection, waiting to give the good news of Christ’s resurrection. Angels even throw us a party when we come to Christ: “In the same way, I tell you, there is rejoicing in the presence of the angels of God over one sinner who repents” (Luke 15:10).

There are a lot of things we don’t know about angels, but we do know God can use angels to help protect us. Ultimately, God is our Protector. Yet that doesn't mean we won't have trouble. David compares our walk with God to a father and son walking together. The father lets his son play and wander a little, but he never lets go of his son's hand: "Though he stumble, he will not fall, for the Lord upholds him with his hand" (Psalm 37:24).

We may stumble through life, wrestle through troubles, but the Lord holds onto our hands.

Taking God with Us

As you go through the day, imagine God walking with you, holding your hand, while angels surround you with protection.

1. Pay attention to the things people around you do in an effort to protect themselves.
2. Where do you feel the safest? Why do you think you feel safe there?

3. Everybody's afraid of something. When do you fear for your own safety? For the safety of others?
4. During the day, think of all the ways God is protecting you. Don't forget to say thanks.

Parting Prayer

Father, thank you for sending your angels to watch us and protect us. Thank you for being our Protector. We're sorry we forget that you look after us minute-by-minute. Help us today to remember you and to think of you holding on to our hands.

Reporting on God's Protection

Give each family member an opportunity to report on God's protection. If you're using these pages as a family journal or record, you might want to keep an ongoing list of "near-misses" to remind you of God's protection.

1. What ideas have you had about angels in the past? What do know about angels now? What don't you know?
2. Talk about times when you've been the most afraid.
3. Think back and remember some of the scares you've had in your family. Accidents? Hospital visits? Illnesses? Did God help you through the crises?
4. Even though God never lets go of our hands, why do you think God lets us stumble?

Are not all angels ministering spirits sent to serve those who will inherit salvation?

—Hebrews 1:14

Day 23

When Jesus was my age, he played a lot with his toys, especially stuffed animals. He just loved stuffed animals.

Krystal, 5

GROWING PAINS

Growing up takes time. The tallest living tree, the Mendocino tree, a coast redwood or Sequoia, near Ukiah, California, measures over 369 feet. It's only taken the tree about 1,000 years to reach this height. The slowest-growing tree is a white cedar on a cliffside in Canada. It grows at a rate of .0003 ounces a year, currently measuring in at .6 ounces and 4 inches tall—all that in only 160 years.

As children grow, approximately 25 percent experience clinical growing pains—aches usually in the muscles of the calves, below the knees, and in front of the thighs. The most intense periods of growing pains occur between the ages of three and five, then again between eight and twelve. According to KidsHealth for Parents, an international health-support organization, the best remedy for a child suffering from growing pains is cuddling.

What God Says

Being confident of this, that he who began a good work in you will carry it on to completion until the day of Christ Jesus.

—Philippians 1:6

The Big Idea

God created us as infants in our mothers' wombs. Physical growth was part of God's plan at creation. So was spiritual growth. If God had wanted to, he could have started us out as adults and given us a mature faith immediately. But growth is an important part of God's plan for us.

Letters written to the Corinthians and to the Hebrews chided the early Christians for their stunted growth. Stuck in spiritual infancy, they still needed spiritual milk, the basics for getting through each day. The letters encouraged readers to grow in faith: "But solid food is for the mature, who by constant use have trained themselves to distinguish good from evil" (Hebrews 5:14). How do we grow spiritually? We train—we exercise the faith we have.

In the Parable of the Four Soils, Jesus compares spiritual growth to the growth of seeds in a farmer's field. The same seed is planted in four different kinds of soil. Some of the seeds get snatched away; some dry up; others get choked by thorns; and some seeds grow and multiply. Jesus explained that the seed is the Word of God in us. We can't make ourselves grow any more than a farmer can make his crop grow. But through confession, through practicing wisdom and kindness, spending time with God, reading the Bible, we can keep our soil a good place for the Word to grow in us.

Taking God with Us

Today, pay attention to the feats your body is able to perform. Then think about your physical and spiritual growth. Try to get a perspective on your life.

1. How have you changed physically over the last five years? Be specific. How would your day today be different if you hadn't changed over the past five years?
2. What spiritual lessons do you seem to have to learn over and over again (spiritual milk)? Think about why you have trouble getting past these lessons.

3. During the day, ask God to show you two ways you've grown spiritually in the past year.
4. How's your spiritual soil? As you go through your day today, keep an eye out for elements that might hamper your spiritual growth.

Parting Prayer

Father, we're sorry that we think about our bodies and how we're growing and changing more than we think about our spiritual growth. We want to grow and have a mature faith. Thank you for planting your seed in us. Help us become the people you created us to be.

Reporting on God's Spiritual Growth

Give each family member an opportunity to report on spiritual growth. One person might record all the responses so you can check back in a month or a year and track your growth.

1. How have you changed physically in the last year? The last five years?
2. How have you grown spiritually over the last year? What specific changes can you see in each other and in your family?
3. Consider the spiritual milk in your life. What lessons do you seem to have to learn over and over again? Why do you think those areas are hard for you?
4. What changes can you make in your family to make the soil of your home more conducive to spiritual growth?

We have much to say about this, but it is hard to explain because you are slow to learn. In fact, though by this time you ought to be teachers, you need someone to teach you the elementary truths of God's word all over again. You need milk, not solid food!

anyone who lives on milk, being still an infant, is not acquainted with the teaching about righteousness.

—Hebrews 5:11–13

HEAVENLY CITIZENS

In order to apply for U.S. citizenship, you have to meet some pretty stiff requirements:

- You must be at least eighteen years old.
- You have to lawfully come into the United States and get permission from the U.S.

Immigration and Naturalization Service to live in this country.

- You must live in the United States at least five years before filing for citizenship.
- You must have "good moral character."
- You have to show that you're attached to the principles of the U.S. Constitution.
- You must take an Oath of Allegiance, promising to bear arms for the United States or perform services for the government when required, if necessary.
- You have to pass a history test.

What God Says

But our citizenship is in heaven. And we eagerly await a Savior from there, the Lord Jesus Christ.

—Philippians 3:20

The Big Idea

To become a citizen of heaven, we believe in Jesus, accepting his death as payment for our sin and believing in the resurrection. We don't pass a test, don't present a list of good works, don't make all kinds of promises.

Jesus told the disciples that he was returning to heaven to get ready for them: "In my Father's house are many rooms; if it were not so, I would have told you. I am going there to prepare a place for you. And if I go and prepare a place for you, I will come back and take you to be with me that you also may be where I am" (John 14:2–3).

While we're living on earth, we need to remember that we're also citizens of heaven. Colossians 3:1–2 says we need to be heaven-minded: "Set your hearts on things above, where Christ is seated at the right hand of God. Set your minds on things above, not on earthly things."

Life is bigger than your town, your country, the world. Don't get earthly tunnel vision.

Thinking more about heaven will make us better citizens of earth, too. We'll see the needs and take the time to help. In fact, living on earth as citizens of heaven makes us ambassadors: "We are therefore Christ's ambassadors, as though God were making his appeal through us. We implore you on Christ's behalf: Be reconciled to God" (II Corinthians 5:20).

We'll be citizens of our country for a long time, but we'll be citizens of heaven for eternity.

Taking God with Us

Today, keep in mind that you have dual citizenship, and you are an ambassador.

1. Keep track of your thoughts during the day. How often do you think about God or heaven? What do you think about most of the time?
2. Pick two heavenly ideas—how God knows everything, or that Jesus died for you, or that Christ is coming back one day. Dwell on those truths all day.
3. Three times today, thank God for your citizenship in heaven.
4. Be an ambassador from heaven today, and talk about Jesus to one person.

Parting Prayer

Father, we're so grateful that Christ died for us and rose from the dead, returning to heaven to make rooms for us. Thank you for forgiving our sins and making us citizens of heaven. Help us take our role as ambassadors seriously.

Reporting on Heaven

Give family members an opportunity to report on things they thought about today. Talk openly about your citizenship in heaven and all that it means.

1. Is everybody confident of his or her citizenship in heaven? Any doubts?
2. What do you think heaven is like? What do you know for sure about heaven?
3. How often did you think about God and heaven today? Where does your mind usually end up?
4. Come up with one way you can be heaven's ambassador tomorrow.

Now we know that if the earthly tent we live in is destroyed, we have a building from God, an eternal house in heaven, not built by human hands.

—II Corinthians 5:1

✳ Day 25 ✳

I don't know why God takes so long to answer your prayers. But he's very old. Maybe he forgets?

Vince, 8

DON'T FORGET

Try this. Everybody close your eyes (OK—except the one reading). If you're in the kitchen, try naming all the objects on top of your fridge or on the counter. Pick another familiar sight if you're somewhere else. Now open your eyes and look around. Did you forget anything?

Can you remember what everyone else in your family wore yesterday? Try it.

Take the penny test:

Which way does the head on a penny face? (How about on a dime? nickel? quarter?)

Does the head on a penny have a beard? Long or short? A tie?

What words are on the front of pennies—all the words?

Where is the date located?

Messages come into our brains continually, traveling at speeds up to two hundred miles an hour. It's impossible to remember every image and message. To make matters worse, we lose about a thousand brain cells a day (out of a quadrillion or so).

Still, the human brain is an amazing work of art and science. Our approximately three-pound brain is the most complex and orderly arrangement of matter known in the universe.

What God Says

We will tell the next generation the praiseworthy deeds of the Lord, his power, and the wonders he has done . . . so the next generation would know them, even the children yet to be born, and they in turn would tell their children. Then they would put their trust in God and would not forget his deeds.

—Psalm 78:4–7

The Big Idea

With the volumes of information bombarding our brains every second, we have to continually select what information will be stored to recall later. Some things have to be forgotten (usually chores like room cleaning), and other things are remembered for life.

Knowing we're forgetful creatures, God has given us reminders. In the Bible, the command to remember occurs 257 times. A rainbow was given to Noah after the flood—a promise and a reminder of God's faithfulness. In Old Testament times, some people carried scripture reminders in phylacteries—little leather boxes strapped to the forehead and the left arm. Other reminders were placed on doorposts of houses or in tassels worn by priests. The feasts, such as Passover, were constant reminders of what God had done for them. In the New Testament, Jesus established the sacrament of Communion: "Do this in remembrance of me."

When Joshua took over for Moses and led the people across the raging Jordan River, he didn't want them to forget the miracle, as they'd forgotten the miracle of the Red Sea crossing. So he sent one person from every tribe back into the river to get rocks and pile them as an altar of remembrance. When they were finished, Joshua explained why they had bothered to pile up the twelve stones: "In the future when your descendants ask their fathers, 'What do these stones mean?' tell them, 'Israel crossed the Jordan on dry ground. For the

Lord your God dried up the Jordan before you until you had crossed over . . . so that all the peoples of the earth might know that the hand of the Lord is powerful'" (Joshua 4:21–24). He wanted the family story passed down so that each generation would remember God's faithfulness and have hope.

We, too, can pass along our own family stories, choosing to remember what God has done for us.

Taking God with Us

Make it a point to remember God today and the things God has done for you.

1. During the day, do you forget anything? What things are easy for you to forget? Why do you think that is?
2. Give yourself a reminder. Instead of tying a string around your finger, come up with another trigger to make you turn your thoughts to God. Today, every

time you see someone wearing red (or hear the word *right* or hear laughter, for example), remember God. Say hi.

3. Today, make it a point to remember and reflect on the blessings and miracles God has done for you over the past year.
4. Choose one moment with God today, an incident or a prayer that you want to remember forever. Go over and over it to embed the experience or thought in your brain.

Parting Prayer

Father, we know how forgetful we can be. Help us to value the right things and appreciate and remember how faithful you are. Give us stories to tell and pass down through generations. Thanks for understanding.

Reporting on Remembering

Give each family member an opportunity to report memories. You might want to start a memory scrapbook, filling it with pictures and stories of God's kindness and faithfulness to your family.

1. What are some of your earliest memories of each other? Why do you think those memories stick in your mind?
2. Take turns telling stories about your past experiences, times when God saw you through troubles.
3. How could the stories help you now?
4. How did the trigger work today? Did you remember God more often throughout the day? Want to try again tomorrow, with the same or a different trigger?

Remember your Creator in the days of your youth.

—Ecclesiastes 12:1

Day 26

People made cars and footballs and television and skates and clothes. So I just thank God for myself, 'cause nobody else could have made me.

Benjamin, 9

GIVE GOD CREDIT

The universe has no end. Our sun is too bright to look at, but Sirius, the brightest star we see at night, gives out twenty-six times more light than the sun.

The earth weighs 6,588,000,000,000,000, 000,000,000,000 tons and gains a few tons every day, from meteor dust settling on the earth's surface. Millions of tons of snow fall each year. Each flake begins as a speck of dust surrounded by water. It changes shape as it collides with other snowflakes. It's true—no two snowflakes are alike.

Three-quarters of the earth is covered by oceans. Scientists used to believe ocean floors (parts of which are six miles deep) were flat. Now they know ocean floors contain mountains and valleys, including a chain of underwater mountains ten thousand miles long in the Atlantic. The Grand Canyon, not the deepest canyon in the United States, could hold the world's population.

Gorillas have unique nose prints (no two are alike). Houseflies have eight thousand eyes. Ants have five noses. Polar bears are left-handed. When diving down on prey, the peregrine falcon can reach two hundred miles per hour. The largest animal is a blue whale (190 tons), and the smallest is plankton, which whales eat. There are over thirty thousand known species of plankton.

If you're not amazed at our world, you're not paying attention.

What God Says

Praise him, sun and moon, praise him, all you shining stars. . . . Praise the Lord from the earth, you great sea creatures . . . you mountains and all hills . . . wild animals . . . small creatures . . . young men and maidens, old men and children. Praise the Lord.

—Psalm 148

The Big Idea

Praise sounds like such a godly and holy activity that it should be reserved for heaven, when we're better equipped. But you praise or get praised every day. Praising is natural. Every time you slap a buddy on the back and say, "Way to go!" that's praise. When someone tells you that you did a good job, that's praise. When you grin thanks for a good dinner, when you exclaim, "Wow!" or when you say, "She did it!" you're praising.

Praise comes from the same root word as *prize* and *price.* It starts with valuing someone else's work, putting a high price on it. God's amazing world is a standing ovation for the Creator. No matter how many sunsets you've watched, how many full moons you see, you should continually be amazed. Place a high price on what God has made and done.

In Deuteronomy, Moses sings praises to the assembly of Israel, encouraging them to ascribe greatness to God or to give God credit for the things God had done. We need to be amazed at the world around us, at all creation. But we have to go a step further and give God, the Creator, due credit.

In Psalm 34:1, David promises: "I will extol the Lord at all times; his praise will always be on my lips." Praising some people can be pretty tough because they're not doing much to congratulate them about. But praising God should be easy. Everything God does is praiseworthy.

Taking God with Us

Today's the day to consciously give God credit for everything around you. Praise him!

1. Be on the lookout today for praise of any kind. Take note every time you hear anybody giving credit and approval to someone else.
2. Try to notice all the praiseworthy creations in nature that you see today. Let yourself say, "Wow!"
3. Are there good things in your life that you haven't given God due credit for? When you think of them today, give God the praise he deserves.
4. Very naturally, tell one friend today something God has done for you or something God has created that you think is awesome.

Parting Prayer

God, we're sorry that we don't always notice the amazing things you do. We don't give you credit often enough. Open our eyes today so that we can see and appreciate your handiwork. Remind us who did it. Teach us how to praise and to never take your gifts for granted.

Reporting on Praise

Give each family member an opportunity to report on the day's praise. You might want to start a "praiseworthy list" and give God credit in writing.

1. Are there things you do or have done that you don't think other people (including the family) give you credit for? How does that make you feel?

2. What examples of ordinary people-to-people praise did you observe or take part in today?
3. Did you give God credit in front of another person today?
4. What things could you give God credit for in your own family? Do it!

Clap your hands, all you nations; shout to God with cries of joy. How awesome is the Lord Most High, the great King over all the earth!

—Psalm 47:1–2

Day 27

Jesus looks like a king and sits in a chair, looking powerful. But don't worry about recognizing him. He'll know who you are.

Pearl, 6

GOD KNOWS

History is filled with secrets. At the end of the fifteenth century, a new fashion took over in England: square-tipped shoes for men, just like Charles VIII's shoes. What the public didn't know was that Charles's shoes were designed to hide his deformity—a sixth toe. French women in Louis XI's court claimed to love only soup, no solid food. Their secret? They were afraid chewing would give them wrinkles.

Three people had similar secrets in the 1860s. Dr. James Barry, a general in Queen Victoria's army, entered the Medical Corps, served forty years as surgeon, and became inspector general of hospitals. Over in America, slim, wiry, Charley Parkhurst became the most famous stagecoach driver in California, while Frank Thompson joined the 2nd Michigan Infantry to fight for the Union in the Civil War. Their shared secret? They were women! Knowing they couldn't do what they wanted to *as women,* Dr. Barry, Charlotte Parkhurst, and Sara Edmonds masqueraded as men.

What God Says

Nothing in all creation is hidden from God's sight. Everything is uncovered and laid bare before the eyes of him to whom we must give account.

—Hebrews 4:13

The Big Idea

God knows us, from the number of hairs on our heads to our deepest thoughts. King David expressed amazement at how thoroughly God knew him: "O Lord, you have searched me and you know me. You know when I sit and when I rise; you perceive my thoughts from afar. Before a word is on my tongue you know it completely, O Lord" (Psalm 139:1–4). David's son Solomon declared, "For you alone know the hearts of all men" (1 Kings 8:39).

But the amazing thing is that, knowing us totally, God still loves us and wants to be our friend! Can you imagine how your friends and family would treat you if they knew you completely—knew every bad thought you've had, including thoughts about them? Jesus knew the disciples completely. But he still called them friends (John 15).

Because God knows us so well, we can be honest with him. At the end of Psalm 139, after David has marveled at how completely God knows him, he says, "Test me and know my anxious thoughts. See if there is any offensive way in me, and lead me in the way everlasting."

Realizing that God knows us intimately and loves us anyway should free us to be honest and open with God. There are no secrets from God.

Taking God with Us

Try to be more honest with God today than you've ever been before.

1. Can you think of three secrets you don't think any living human being knows about you? Talk to God about those secrets today.
2. Today, notice thoughts you have about other people. Keep track of some of those thoughts that you'd hate for other people to know about.

3. Who's the one person on earth you think knows you best? Make a mental list of all the things that person does not know about you.
4. Ask God to show you something new about yourself today, something you may not have admitted to yourself before.

Parting Prayer

Father, we're not sure how to feel about the fact that we don't have a single secret from you. We're sorry for all the things we thought we were getting away with. Thank you for loving us anyway and for still wanting to be our friend. Help us to be honest with you.

Reporting on Friendship with God

Give each family member an opportunity to talk about his or her friendship with God. You may or may not want to share secrets.

1. Can you share any thoughts you had about other people today—thoughts you're glad they didn't overhear?
2. How does it make you feel to know that God knows everything about you?
3. Why do you think God still wants to be friends, even when he knows your deepest secrets and thoughts?
4. How could you be more honest with God?

Surely you desire truth in the inner parts.
—Psalm 51:6

Day 28

Once upon a time, God got bored up in heaven by hisself. It was too dull. So he got this great idea. God made us! He's very creative that way.

Lara, 8

GOD'S MASTERPIECES

You've probably heard of masterpieces like the Mona Lisa and The Last Supper. But have you heard of John Banyard's masterpiece? In 1846, he finished the largest manmade painting in the world. The twelve-foot-wide canvas ran three miles long, depicting the countryside from a twelve-hundred-mile stretch from the mouth of the Mississippi to New Orleans. It was exhibited on a moving screen, pulling the canvas through. The whole show took two hours.

Sara Winchester of San Jose, California, created a strange masterpiece: the Winchester House, with 160 rooms, 8 stories, 48 fireplaces, many miles of secret passages, 2,000 doors, and 10,000 windows.

Hobbyists all over the world prize their own collections, even if no one else does. Gary Duschl of Ontario began his gum-wrapper chain in 1965; it's over 26,000 feet long now. A man in Arkansas has collected over 7,000 four-leaf clovers. A woman in Queens has over 700 Pez candy dispensers. One person's junk is another guy's masterpiece.

What God Says

For we are God's workmanship [masterpieces], created in Christ Jesus.

—Ephesians 2:10

The Big Idea

God created us, and we are his masterpieces. He doesn't just love us in theory, from far away. He cares actively. We're valuable to him, his glorious inheritance (Ephesians 1:18). And we're his children: "How great is the love the Father has lavished on us, that we should be called children of God!" (I John 3:1).

God takes delight in his masterpieces, in us; "For the Lord takes delight in his people" (Psalm 149:4). He's preoccupied with us, thinking about us night and day, caring for us and listening to us because he loves us so much.

Have you ever seen brand-new parents? They can usually be identified by the thousands of baby pictures they carry with them. They talk nonstop about all the amazing things their babies can do. They delight in those kids. The same thing probably goes on in your family, too. We know it goes on in

God's family. God delights in us. He can't get enough.

Jesus told the disciples, "As the Father has loved me, so have I loved you" (John 15:9). There could be no greater love than the love between God the Father and God the Son, but Jesus says he loves us that much. Jesus loves me. This I know.

Taking God with Us

Today, hold your head high and smile. Remember that God is delighting in you. You are God's masterpiece.

1. During the day, notice the things that delight people (including you). What kinds of things do most people consider masterpieces?
2. What's the closest thing you have to a masterpiece, something you think is amazing?

3. During the day, whenever you don't feel like a masterpiece, picture God smiling proudly at you, delighting in you.

4. The Bible says that God hears our every sigh. Let sighs be your memory cue for the day. When you sigh or hear someone else sigh, talk to God. Thank him for loving you so much.

Parting Prayer

Father, we can't imagine why you think so much of us, but we feel your delight. Help us to see ourselves through your eyes. We know we're nothing without Christ, but you count us your masterpieces. Thanks for claiming us as your children. We love you and delight in you, too.

Reporting on God's Delight

Help each other feel like masterpieces as you talk. You might create a "verbal family portrait," filling it with good things God says about you.

1. When you daydream and your thoughts turn to something cool, what do you think about?
2. Name some things you take delight in. What are your masterpieces?
3. What things did you sigh about today? Did you imagine God smiling and listening?
4. Talk about low moments—times you definitely do not feel like a masterpiece. Could it help at those times to remember what God says about you?

He brought me out into a spacious place;
he rescued me because he delighted in me.
—II Samuel 22:20

Day 29

In heaven you can eat all the candy you want and you don't get fat or cavities.

Owen, 10

UPSIDE-DOWN AND INSIDE-OUT!

People have nearly always obsessed over weight, hair, and makeup. The ancient Assyrians cut their hair in the shape of pyramids. In ancient Rome, men sometimes painted hair onto their bald heads; Grecian women preferred wearing live cicadas as hair ornaments. Women in seventeenth-century

France often piled their hair several feet up, decorating it with models of Paris, windmills, and waterfalls. English men during the reign of Elizabeth I sometimes slept with beard presses clamped to their beards at night to keep every hair in place.

In China, noblemen used to paint dark rings around their eyes to make themselves more handsome. Some of them grew their fingernails as long as they could and topped them off with golden nail guards. Catherine de Medici, who lived in sixteenth-century Italy, always washed her face with a mixture of crushed almonds and peach blossoms picked at dawn. Queen Isabeau of fourteenth-century Bavaria made her own skin lotion—a mixture of boar's brains, crocodile glands, and wolf blood.

What God Says

Your beauty should not come from outward adornment, such as braided hair and the wearing of gold jewelry and fine clothes.

Instead, it should be that of your inner self, the unfading beauty of a gentle and quiet spirit, which is of great worth in God's sight.

—I Peter 3:3–4

The Big Idea

When Saul was King of Israel, God told the prophet Samuel it was time to anoint another king, one who would love God with his whole heart. So God sent Samuel to Bethlehem, to the home of Jesse to anoint one of Jesse's sons. One by one, seven strong sons were marched past Samuel, but God said no to each one. Confused, Samuel asked Jesse if he had any more sons, and Jesse confessed that there was the youngest, still out tending sheep. When young David joined them, God told Samuel to anoint him as king, even though he was smaller than the other brothers, because, "The Lord does not look at the things man looks at. Man looks at the outward appearance, but the Lord looks at the heart" (I Samuel 16:7). God cares more about what's inside of us than what we look like on the outside.

Looking inside-out isn't the only topsy-turvy thing about God's perspective. He tells you to turn the other cheek, to give your shirt to the thief who stole your coat, to love your enemies and pray for people who persecute you, to be glad when people say bad things about you, to return good for evil. In God's upside-down world, a King is born in a stable, we lose our life to gain it, when we're weak we're strong, the greatest will be the least, and the last will be first.

Taking God with Us

Take a fresh look at the world around you today, and try to get a clearer vision of the things that are important to God.

1. How much time do you spend on your outside, trying to make a good impression today?
2. What do you do during the day to take care of your insides, your spiritual nature and character?
3. Try to pretend that everyone around you looks pretty much the same and is equally popular. What differences can you detect on the inside?
4. Do one upside-down thing today—choosing to go last or to serve, for instance.

Parting Prayer

God, help us to see the world the way you do. It's your world, and our own selfishness has flipped it upside-down. Help us to be more concerned with the kind of people we're becoming than with our physical appearance. We want to be like you on the inside.

Reporting on God's Upside-Down World

Let each family member discuss the way God sees things and the way the world sees things. You might want to start an "upside-down list."

1. Normally, how much time do you spend on your outside, versus your inside?
2. How can we spend more time developing our inside, our spirits?
3. Try to make sense out of some of the upside-down comments in the Bible. What does it mean for the last to be first? How are we strongest when we're weak?
4. Do you care more about what's inside a person or what that person looks like? Consider the friends you've chosen and the people you most want to be like.

Dress modestly, with decency and propriety, not with braided hair or gold or pearls or expensive clothes, but with good deeds.

—I Timothy 2:9

Day 30

God is really, really, really, really old. And he never looks a day older every time you see him.

Nate, 6

EYE-OPENERS: BELIEVING IS SEEING

Birds see everything at once in total focus. A bird's eye is flat and can take in everything in a single glance. Our eyes, on the other hand, are round and have to refocus for different distances.

If you can leave the flashlight at home and keep outside lights off, your eye will adjust to the night, making your eyesight as perceptive as the owl's, at least for a while. And on a clear, moonless night, the human eye should be able to see a match being struck as far as fifty miles away. On the first orbited flight, astronauts were astounded that they could see the wake of ships in earth's oceans.

The easiest color to see is a particular shade of yellow-green, which is the exact shade of a forest canopy. But some people go through life colorblind, unable to tell one color from another.

And here's a little trick you can try. If you want to know whether someone is truly interested in what you're saying or is maybe just faking it, watch the pupils of the eyes. Pupils dilate when someone is interested. The eyes tell all!

What God Says

Then Jesus told him [Thomas], "Because you have seen me, you have believed; blessed are those who have not seen and yet have believed."

—John 20:29

The Big Idea

When the King of Aram was at war with Israel, he became furious with the prophet Elisha for constantly tipping off the Israeli king as to where Aram planned to attack next. Finally, the king sent an army with horses and chariots to surround the city of Dothan, where Elisha and his servant were staying. When Elisha's servant saw the army who had come up against them, he was terrified. But Elisha told him not to be afraid. They had the king's troops outnumbered. Elisha prayed, "O Lord, open his eyes so he may see." Then the Lord opened the servant's eyes, and he looked and saw the hills full of horses and chariots of fire all around Elisha, (II Kings 6:17). God was protecting them, but they had to open their eyes to see it.

After Jesus' resurrection, two of his disciples were walking on the road to Emmaus, talking about everything that had happened, when Jesus walked up and joined the discussion. The men didn't recognize Jesus as he explained to them how the prophecies of scripture had been fulfilled in Christ's death and resurrection. Later they ate together, and Jesus broke the bread and gave thanks for their meal. And that's when it happened: "Then their eyes were opened and they recognized him" (Luke 24:31). Jesus had been with them all along, but they couldn't see it.

God is with us, too, all the time. Open your eyes and see.

Taking God with Us

See if today you can believe what you can't see with your eyes.

1. Today, keep track of all the things you automatically believe without seeing (electricity, wind, and so on).
2. In the middle of a noisy moment today, stop. Realize that God is with you. Whisper to him.
3. Are there any times when you're more aware of Christ's presence than other times?
4. What are some other things God might want you to see today?

Parting Prayer

Father, thanks for always being with us and for protecting us wherever we go. Open our eyes to the spiritual world going on around us, to things we can't see. Help us believe and see you in everything.

Reporting on Eyesight

Give each family member an opportunity to report on the seen and the unseen. Use this time to plan how you can continue to grow together in faith.

1. What were some of the ordinary things you believed in today, without seeing?
2. What do you think it means to be spiritually blind? Do you think you have great spiritual eyesight or a touch of blindness?
3. What do you think is going on around you right now, unseen? What could you do to improve your spiritual vision?
4. Discuss together any insights you've gained over the past thirty days. What changes do you want to work on together?

I pray also that the eyes of your heart may be enlightened in order that you may know the hope to which he has called you.

—Ephesians 1:18

✳ The Author ✳

Dandi Daley Mackall has published about 330 books for kids and grown-ups. She has also written articles for *Today's Woman, Western Horseman, Cowboy Hall of Fame, Chicken Soup for the Kid's Soul, Family Circle, Parenting, Worldwide Challenge, Guideposts, Power for Living,* and other publications. She has produced a humor column and served as freelance editor. She's a frequent guest on radio talk shows, has hosted many radio phone-in programs, and made dozens of appearances on television. She was an instructor for a *Highlights* conference and teaches novel writing for the Institute of Children's Literature.

Dandi conducts writing assemblies and workshops across the United States and gives keynotes at conferences and Young Author events. She writes from rural Ohio, with husband, Joe; children, Jen, Katy, and Dan; horses, dogs, and cats.

You can write to Dandi at
www.dandibooks.com